The Progressive Gene

How Genetics Influence the Morality of the Left

The Progressive Gene

How Genetics Influence the Morality of the Left

Michael C. Anderson

Simms Books Publishing

SIMMS BOOKS PUBLISHING

Publishers Since 2012

Published By Simms Books Publishing

Jonesboro, GA

Library of Congress Cataloging in Publication Data
2017918451

Michael C. Anderson

The Progressive Gene

How Genetics Influences the Morality of the Left

ISBN:978-0-9996882-0-5

Printed in the United States of America

Book Arrangement by Simms Books Publishing

Cover Art Shelly Anderson/Urias Brown

Mary Hoekstra- Editor

DEDICATION

To Jonathan Haidt, who showed me the way.

ACKNOWLEDGEMENTS

I am grateful to the following people who helped me complete this project:

Mary Hoekstra, my tireless and ruthless editor, who challenged me to be better,

Ellen Loeffler-Kalinoski, my photographer, and Shelly Anderson, my graphic designer.

TABLE OF CONTENTS

PREFACE

This book wrote itself. I didn't, at least not consciously. All I did was press the keys to put the words on paper. My words are a direct expression of my growing concern over the state of American politics. That concern began with the election of Barack Obama and the reestablishment of the Progressive narrative. Or maybe it goes back farther than that, perhaps with the hanging chad election of George Bush. That election motivated the Left and help set up the opportunity for Obama to win.

As a person who is more comfortable on the political Right than the Left, I try to maintain objectivity about politics for two reasons. First, no political group or party is capable of presenting solutions that are consistently better than the opposition. Both sides strive to make their belief system acceptable to the American people, so they can rise to power and take control of the federal government. Each side is equally selfish and power hungry so the agenda of each needs to be moderated. When either has control, moderation is discarded, and those with the power move farther away from the center. Democrats try to expand the welfare state. Republicans try to dismantle it. Usually control does not stay with one party too long, because the American people tire of the incumbents and want to try someone else.

What concerns me now is the Progressive control of the media, which started in the Bush years and has carried through the Obama presidency. Because the twenty-four-hour media has such enormous influence, and leans Left, Progressives dominate the airwaves with their talking points. We have seen the Progressive belief system at work in every aspect of American society, whether it be an emphasis on secularization (ex. can't say "Merry Christmas"), attacks on Capitalism as evil, creation of an "us versus them" narrative pitting those with relatively low incomes against high wage earners (wage envy), same-sex marriage initiatives, and the fifteen dollar minimum wage. This belief system has been operating for over one hundred years, but the difference this time is the media's ability to control what we hear. Conservatives and constituencies associated with them, like white working-class men, are regarded as either ignorant or stupid. They exist as Hillary's "deplorables". In addition, stay at home moms are considered misguided slaves to their husbands, when they should be building a career. Only dopes go to church.

This distortion of reality can destroy the American culture when there is too much emphasis on what groups want and no emphasis on what American needs.

What we should be doing is looking for the best course of action that is practical and makes sense for the whole country, rather than just a few special interest groups. The United States has some three hundred million citizens, and 40% of that number supports each of the major political parties. If we want to move forward, we'll have to move together. Two minorities with diverging positions do not a majority make. Permanent deadlock is not an option. There are problems to solve.

For this book, I created the label "Progressive Gene" to refer to the genetic predisposition of the political Left toward their belief system. As we will discuss later, Progressives have specific characteristics that we can observe: a narrow set of moral foundations causing an outsized focus on caring and fairness, a utopian point of view, a strong affinity to academia as a solver of all problems, and an idealistic belief in government as a change agent.

Like many people, I have been perplexed by the polarization of politics in the United States and unable to make sense of it. Things that seemed obvious to me seem to escape the radar of politicians. For example, those on the Left never seem to worry about bankrupting the country. They are willing to make the welfare state as big as it needs to be to take care of everyone. Don't they understand how inefficient bureaucracies are? The Right, on the other hand, is criticized for being heartless and uncaring. Odd that they never seem to answer the charge, even verbally. Most of what comes out of the Republican establishment resembles the nineteenth century concept of social Darwinism.

When I read Jonathan Haidt's book, *The Righteous Mind: Why Good People are Divided by Politics and Religion* (2012), a light turned on. Suddenly, everything made sense to me. Haidt has built on previous research to show that human beings have a set of innate moral foundations that have become part of our DNA over the past 200,000 years of human existence. These foundations include caring, fairness, loyalty, authority, sanctity, and liberty. What's most interesting about these traits is that they are not doled out in equal proportion to people. Everyone gets a unique mix. For example, I may be more caring than you, you may be more loyal than me.

The implications of Haidt's work are profound. First, his work has strengthened the argument that morality is relative. Despite their hard labor, every philosopher since the Greeks has wasted their time trying to find absolute morality. Religion depends on absolutes too, because the dogma is the set of rules for all to live by. How can you have dogma when morality is relative? Now, let's not go too far with this. You are going to say that if morality is relative, laws don't mean anything, and we can do what suits us as individuals. If my morality says stealing is ok, then I can steal.

However, in society, there are two moralities, not one. Individual morality and societal morality. Individual morality is the morality of family; how we live our lives to protect our family and offspring. Societal morality is the rulebook for human beings to live together in large groups. Through most of the history of mankind, we lived in egalitarian groups of 50-150 individuals. This is an expression of our innate social behavior. But the advent of agriculture provided us with enough food to support a larger concentration of people, so man could abandon a nomad's life. Larger groups required a new morality; one that could be used to manage a group, was hierarchical, and stratified by social and economic status.

Government is the enforcer of the group morality, protecting us and helping stimulate and stabilize our economic environment. Government extends morality through laws, so if you want to live in society, you agree to obey the laws. Those who do not accept them, go to jail.

If you dig into Haidt's work, you discover another very interesting thing. Haidt graphed the strength of each human moral foundation, obtained from surveying individuals, against its position on the political spectrum. Progressive zealots on the Left; Conservative zealots on the Right; and Independents in the middle. The graphs clearly show that conservatives and liberals have a different morality. When I looked at the characteristics of Progressives, those individuals to Left of the Liberals in the Democratic Party, another light went on. I had been confused about Progressives attitudes toward the disadvantaged, and their support of the welfare state, but now it all made sense. Progressives have an outsized caring and fairness morality, which drives them to have empathy for the "helpless" and a feeling that helping them is a fundamental requirement of society. This is an expression of the Progressive Gene at work.

For reasons that will probably never be known, Progressive morality is not as balanced as morality at the other end of the political spectrum. I am not being judgmental about this distinction; you can check it yourself by looking at Haidt's graphs. I am not saying that Conservatives have better morals or are more righteous than Progressives. What I am saying is that those on the Right, as the result of a more balanced set of moral foundations, need to reconcile their morality in a way that Progressives don't, and this leads them to a different position on political issues. Let's return to economic equality as an example. Progressives look that this issue solely from a caring/fairness standpoint. To them, inequality produces poverty, which is unfair to the poor as citizens. Their care foundation feels for the suffering of others, and they want to alleviate it.

Conservatives take a wider view of poverty problem. Is it fair to take my money and give it to someone else; money I've earned by working hard? Doesn't that violate my rights and deny me liberty? What if the money the government takes from me is misused? Then, my right to the pursuit of happiness has been violated with no intended outcome. Conservatives will support welfare that requires participation of the recipients, wanting assurances those receiving aid are trying to develop a skill, or get a job.

The variation in human morality creates problems when it comes to developing a consensus about the role of government; because the political mood of the country swings back and forth from Right to Left. Often, the pendulum spends too much time at one end or the other without spending enough time in the middle. You would have to do some research to find a period in American history with as much divisiveness as we have today. The pendulum, despite Donald Trump's victory, is firmly on the Left.

Regardless of varied views of morality, Americans need to come together to solve the enormous problems we face. The Right and the Left need to figure out how to compromise and work together or the country will not move forward. America is becoming more diverse, and with diversity comes the conflict of adaptation, so we had better try to figure out how to balance unity with diversity. If that balance is missing and the glue that unifies us disappears, we become weaker as a nation.

What this book is about...

Explaining the unique morality of the Progressives and how it has been influenced by biology, group morality, and the history of governments.

Describing American history since the colonial time: the principles that created our nation, how the federal government achieved legitimacy, and the way the colonial experience is infused in the American character.

Presenting the history of the Progressive movement: why it came into being and what it has been able to accomplish.

Discussing the Progressive Movement of today; its objectives, the plan for achieving those objectives, and whether it is possible to achieve them in a way that benefits the American people.

CHAPTER ONE

TURMOIL IN AMERICAN POLITICS

Increasingly, the picture of our society as rendered in our media is illusionary and delusionary: disfigured, unreal, out of touch with reality, disconnected from the true context of our life. It is disfigured by celebrity, by celebrity worship, by gossip, by sensationalism, by denial of our societies.

Carl Bernstein

We are six months past the 2016 presidential election and the American political system has been in turmoil ever since. The election of Donald Trump marked the end of one of the most divisive presidential elections in the history of our republic. In this case, the public was looking for change and a populist Republican sensed it. The Democrats abandoned one of their core constituencies and ran a muddled campaign about issues that didn't ignite passion. Meanwhile, a Socialist, third party candidate morphed himself into a Democrat. By appealing to the disillusionment of the millennial generation, he almost stole the Democratic show. Quite a year.

This last election signaled a halt to the ascendancy of the Progressive wing of the Democratic Party. Their message had been carried by the Obama Administration's for eight years, although his disinterest in compromise contributed to the polarization of government and fostered a Republican "do nothing but resist" agenda. Even without control of the presidency, the Progressives continue their march forward, propped up by the media, which broadcasts their ideology across the globe. Right now, the Progressives seem intent on adopting the Republican's stonewall tactics, so we will have to see where that leads.

At the center of this post-election maelstrom is an impotent federal government stifled by political ideologues that put their beliefs, and the beliefs of their most vocal constituents, ahead of the country. Polls judging the effectiveness of Congress run steadily in the mid-teens, and are among the lowest of all American institutions. Congress is motivated by lobbyists, not polls.

America is moving toward an oligarchy in which a few people and their groups control the direction of the country at-large. Money flows from the elite class through lobbyists, who pull the strings of the politicians. Republicans, who are in the majority, have as much trouble getting consensus within their own party as they have trying to work with Democrats. Their renegade faction, the Tea Party, sees all legislative action through the lens of fiscal control, and will not compromise under any circumstances. Their zeal mimics that of the Progressives who stick to their ideology through thick and thin.

Within the political spectrum, Progressives as the most liberal faction, gather on the Left, proliferating the welfare state, big government programs, and socio-economic equality. Their agenda is "idealistic" because it assumes all problems in society are solved with more government. On the Right are the Conservatives, dedicated to their perception of the American ideal of individualism as originally defined in the Constitution. Conservatives generally oppose the Progressives' welfare state as wasteful and inefficient. They also resist any change, worrying that an unknown path might destabilize the country.

The American Progressive movement was born during the closing decades of the 19th Century and arose again late in the 20th Century as a re-defined, re-packaged replacement for Liberalism. The latter had failed in practice and soiled its name for posterity. Because Liberalism failed to deliver, the ideologues of the Democratic Party were compelled to adopt the Progressive "label" and definitions for their philosophy of government. This re-messaging worked in the two elections won by Obama, in 2008 and 2012, when Progressives gained control of the White House.

Progressives maintain the political narrative today because their messaging about social and economic equality fits with the times. This is an age of increased sensitivity and awareness of evil throughout the world. There is a constant stream of news stories, every hour, every day, describing the suffering, which overexposes us to pain and suffering. This inescapable awareness works on the Progressives' innate mindset and moves them into action against causes of inequality.

The importance of Progressive ideas in our culture is beyond debate; they serve to challenge the status quo, incubate innovative ideas to push society forward, and act as tireless champions for equality. Political and philosophical balance within a society is as important as innovation, however, and history clearly shows that a consensus of ideas has the best chance to propel society forward. When the pendulum swings too far to one side of the ideological spectrum, and only one position dominates, the results are disruptive, or worse.

In the past, Americans shared a unifying set of beliefs: love of country; respect for the military; setting an example for the world; desire for one's children to receive the best education; and the achievement of a lifestyle better than that of the previous generation. Those beliefs cut across all stripes; we created and shared a kinship of purpose as Americans. While the influx of new Americans came from Western Europe, the belief system remained intact. In the last fifty years, our population has become more heterogeneous; immigration of non-Western European ethnic groups has increased, and these groups represent cultures with different beliefs.

Our former unity is challenged by the growing emphasis on groups previously disadvantaged in our society, such as African Americans, women, members of the LGBTQ community, who now strive to be recognized as equals in all aspects of American life. Social equality has become a front and center political objective of the Progressives. The unfortunate consequence of diversity is that it divides rather than unifying through emphasis on uniqueness and differences, rather than commonality. But this reality is not important to those seeking a status denied them in the past. Their level of enthusiasm and motivation toward the long sought-after goal is what drives them.

An increasing emphasis on group identity distracts from issues that affect the whole country. As a result, individual Americans have become a composite of attributes representing their physical, mental, and social characteristics, rather than a whole American. A female member of a minority group might focus on gender and minority group issues, rather than on American issues. A gay man who wants to get married is more likely to focus on his gender issues more than on being an American. The accomplishments of diversity, though important, are less spectacular if national unity is a casualty of the process.

As Robert Putnam, professor of Public Policy at Harvard has shown, communities with more diversity have less trust between and within ethnic groups, making unity more difficult to achieve.

Separate from the current debate about diversity, there is also a Progressive push to recognize economic equality as a fundamental goal for America. This focuses on the lower socio-economic portion of our population, not just the chronically poor, but also all who might be limited by their circumstances from achieving the American dream. The villains in this Progressive scenario are the wealthy and high wage earners, who have an unfair advantage they use to accumulate more. A commonly discussed metric these days is the wealth and income of the top one percent of the population. Since that group controls 40% of the country's wealth, it seems logical to the Progressives that the government should take some of their money and redistribute it to those who have less and need more. This economic leveling is supposed to make the bottom half of the population happier.

The media have always loved any story that generates advertising dollars, but now they must find enough content to fill a twenty-four-hour news cycle. The truth is, major news events occupy only a small part of the day; the rest of the time consisting of inconsequential, useless and gossip-based information. Not only is content recycled *ad nauseam*, but also the American people have been recruited as unpaid news providers. See something interesting? Like a dog doing tricks? Snap a picture. Witness a crime? Record a video and send it in.

By nature, media gives airtime to the most extreme political views and their emphasis is to the Left of the political center. Each network has panels of experts who parse every word politicians say, and then tell the rest of us what they meant. Joseph Goebbels, Hitler's propaganda minister, once said, "Tell someone the same lie enough times and they will come to believe it." The lies we hear from the media today are veiled in repetition. We hear only the voices of the outliers instead of the majority. The frequent, repetitive reporting of extreme points of view makes it appear that the outliers are the majority, when, in fact, they are not. This drumbeat of repetition hammers on the public who harden their beliefs out of fear. For example, if I think the country is drifting toward Communism and I'm Conservative, my resolve grows stronger. If I'm on the Left and abhor corporate greed, I'm going to harden my belief that capitalism is corrupt.

There is another problem with the twenty-four-hour news cycle; scouring for news drives the media to gather minute details about people, principally those who are well known... movie stars, corporate leaders, politicians and the like. Their activities, minute-by-minute, are fair game, especially when they exhibit behaviors that are questionable, novel, or sensational. Thanks to this non-journalistic approach to news, privacy no longer exists.

In the past, important positions in government, like the Presidency, were respected, no matter who occupied the office. When the President's politics was different from ours, we agreed to disagree. Now, Presidents are commonly called names and ridiculed. Respect is lost everywhere in our society, the exceptions being professions with very strong "protector" identities, such as those in the military and first responders. Police officers used to be part of the admired group but recent abuses, although a small percentage of cases, have harmed their historically admired status. Athletes can also be included in the "admired professions" group but they fall into a special category. Their talent and accomplishments feed into a loyalty emotion that is part of human group behavior, and so their shortcomings as role models are often overlooked or forgiven.

Those outside the respected professions are ridiculed when their views do not match those of a specific group; that is a direct consequence of this loss of respect and disloyalty. Only charisma, as a personal attribute, can generate respect on its own; it can carry a person forward to success. Take the example of President Obama: seven years as state senator in Illinois; four years as United States Senator from Illinois; and then President. Obama lacked the basic qualifications to be President, but his personal charisma got him the votes. He is just one example of the "cult of personality" that enables charismatic individuals to command the attention of those who are easily influenced. A recent poll conducted by *Readers Digest*[1], which identified the one hundred most trusted people in America, had actors in the first four positions.

In addition to the old media, we now have the internet to help accelerate a decline in the quality of news reporting. The internet has no rules and no conscience, so there is no requirement to verify the accuracy of the information that is thrown at us every day. Anyone posting on the internet can call himself a journalist if he chooses, so traditional news organizations, faced with this new competition, lower their journalistic standards to maintain market share. The truth gets lost along the way. "Fake news" has become the popular term *du jour*, and there is *angst* about it. Recently, the large social sites like Facebook have been implementing codes to identify and remove fake news from their sites to protect us from misinformation. How do they know what information is fake? Shouldn't we be smart enough to identify reliable sources of information without Big Brother taking care of that for us?

The polarization of politics and an uncontrolled media have come together to confuse the electorate and help create a crisis of ineffectiveness in government. Congress can only be effective when its members work together on issues and reach a compromise. When they do not, the only winners are the lobbyists, who are rewarded handsomely for blocking legislation that threatens their agendas.

How do we solve this polarization problem? By drawing attention to the risks polarization creates; by identifying its extremist elements; and by making the case that the extremes are detrimental to the future of our society. We need to speak out and debate political philosophies, so we can form a new consensus about the direction our country should take, and we should identify the outliers for what they are – small minorities with extremist views.

Democracy is having its season in the sun now, while other government forms have lost favor. It is regarded as the best chance to balance liberty, freedom, and human rights against the power of government. True democracy, as the Greeks originally envisioned and enacted it, could not exist in today's world because the public cannot be assembled to vote on legislation. Our modern version uses elected representatives to protect the people's interests. This model is beneficial when it is working properly because the apparatus of government can distill the irrational behavior of the public. Elected representatives, through their credentials, bring subject knowledge to their roles and can act as better stewards than the people could be for the direction of the political system. Unfortunately, representatives can become corrupt when others with money influence their votes.

We live in a time when "liberalization" of social behavior is changing the perception of government's role in society. This phenomenon is another reason for changes in attitudes about diversity and the role of government. At this point in the 21st Century, the Progressives have helped things along by reinterpreting the Constitution. Our founding document was built on the concept of rights designed to protect the individual from government. For example, freedom of speech protects any individual from prosecution, no matter what words he may utter. The Progressives have waged a relentless attack on the concept of individual rights because in their view, those stand in the way of efforts to expand the role of government. Group rights protections mandate that the government take the role of caretaker and enforcer.

This Progressive attack on the Constitution has two points of focus. First, as the Progressives assert, the Constitution is archaic and irrelevant because it was written by a group of rich aristocratic landowners who didn't care about the disadvantaged and were only interested in protecting their own property rights from interference by the British government. Second, Progressives have embarked on a well-designed judicial effort that interprets and equates social justice issues as group rights. That means when a group right conflicts with the Constitution, the Constitution must give way. In that interpretation, government protection of homosexuals, same sex marriage, women's rights, equal pay, worker's rights, and fair wages is part of a new social morality.

Changing the Constitution is one of the pillars of the Progressive agenda; the others being a dependence on science as a problem solver and the expansion of the welfare state. They have been successful at deploying this model, despite discouraging results. Still, they keep moving forward. It remains for those who oppose Progressive positions to fight for a balance in political philosophy that can protect the interests of all the American people.

CHAPTER TWO

THE PROGRESSIVE GENE

Morality binds and blinds. It binds us into teams…but thereby makes us go blind to objective reality.

Jonathan Haidt

Man is unique among the world's species; he has evolved into an intelligent, social, and moral being by the forces of natural selection. This process has given him a set of behaviors derived from the creatures that came before him, layer upon layer, vertebrate to mammal, to primate to Hominid. The term "lizard brain" refers to the part of the human brain that drives our instinct for survival, but man has evolved far beyond the reptiles. His complex thinking brain includes morality as a core component of human personality. Morality is a dynamic belief system containing a set of behaviors that allow us to function in a group and adapt to living in human society.

Human beings did not evolve to live in cities. They evolved to live in egalitarian groups like our closest relatives, the Chimpanzees. As the human brain developed beyond those of other species, the course of man's future changed. Man learned to use his brain to control access to food and improve his chances for survival. Later, the advent of agriculture required the development of a human organization that could support a high population density.

A division of labor emerged along with what we know now as socio-economic classes. Where there was social hierarchy, government followed, and the first political systems came into existence.

Governments have always been experiments in balancing a social hierarchy with distributed rights while meeting the needs of individuals and groups who exercise those rights. All political systems have factions that disagree over the role of government and that is true whether it was ancient Greece, Rome, Mesopotamia, or Europe and the United States today. Those factions, through history, demonstrated the variation in human belief about what constitutes good government. Some embrace conservative principles that desire the status quo while others believe in a more dynamic, constantly changing society that requires government efforts to make "improvements".

In a political society, individual morality becomes group morality so the direction a society takes is a consequence of the dominant group morality at any given time. For example, the concept of Eugenics, a method of birth planning to limit the mentally and physically incompetent, was a popular social concept in the United States prior to World War II. When the world witnessed the horrors of Nazi atrocities perpetrated by a diabolical belief in racial superiority, Eugenics was discarded as a desirable social objective. In a similar fashion, the acceptance of homosexuality gained momentum in the late 1980s and is now a fundamental component of the social justice morality accepted in the United States. Because the morality of individuals is variable, and not absolute, the morality of society results from a mixture of individual moralities. Variation in morality is the principle cause of factionalism in politics.

Over the past twenty years, Jonathan Haidt, a contemporary thinker and professor of social psychology, has conducted research designed to answer questions such as: how is it possible for people to have a moral philosophy at odds with their friends and neighbors? How is this variation in human morality consistent with the concept of a single moral standard? In his book, *The Righteous Mind: Why Good People are Divided by Politics and Religion* (2012), Haidt describes how the results of his research drove him to an understanding of the factors that contribute to the development of morality in man and how that morality influences our political views. More importantly, he demonstrated that the foundations of one's morality are not strictly based on learned behaviors but also include the behavioral expression of innate personality traits. Those traits are genetically determined so human morality is, to some degree, hard-wired in the human brain. This innate morality evolved over thousands of generations because it improved man's chances for survival.

Haidt observed that the moral beliefs of a group of individuals he labeled WEIRD -- western, educated, industrial, rich, and democratic – were different from the beliefs of other groups. He concluded that WEIRDs see the world as made up of individuals, which made them focus on protecting individual rights. Non-WEIRD people, by contrast, are more focused on relationships, groups, and institutions so their moral views are more related to group factors. Haidt saw this variation as proof that no single moral view is absolute to the exclusion of all others. In other words, he realized morality is relative.

Professor Haidt identified six moral foundations for human behavior. Caring and fairness are universally recognized, but along with them come loyalty, authority, sanctity, and liberty. Caring means a response to the suffering of others. Fairness means cooperation without taking advantage.

Loyalty describes a person's behavior in a group and the ability to adhere to the goals of the group before attending to personal goals. Authority means adapting to a social hierarchy. Sanctity refers to our "behavioral immune system," which is what makes us wary of things that can be physically threatening. The liberty foundation is invoked when humans feel compelled to resist oppressive authority.

Caring

Without doubt, caring is the strongest and most important moral foundation of human behavior. Mothers have caring instincts to protect and raise their children, and those with the strongest instincts improve the odds of offspring survival. Fathers, who contribute their own caring instincts, improve the odds still further. A thousand generations of natural selection have strengthened and concentrated this emotion. We see examples of caring every day and we respond to sensory triggers that evoke caring and move humans to action. Examples include the sight and sound of infants in distress, people of a community pulling bricks and metal off their neighbors after an earthquake, and most recently, the faces and voices of survivors and victims of terrorism.

Fairness

At first glance, fairness doesn't seem to fit the profile of traits that promote offspring survival because it requires altruistic behavior toward non-family members. Evolutionary biologists have solved that paradox by identifying a link between altruism and human memory. If a person can remember who returned favors and who did not, he can give favors to those individuals who will

14

reciprocate and withhold favors for those who will not reciprocate. In today's political climate, fairness means something different to those on the Right and to those on the Left. To those on the Right, fairness means proportionality or payback for expended effort; to those on the Left, it means equality of opportunity and outcome.

Loyalty

The loyalty foundation, like caring, is deep and fundamental to human behavior. Researchers, in the social sciences, have shown that human beings like to form groups (tribes) and compete against other groups. In the early days of human existence, this tribalism had value. If men wanted to kill large animals, they had to hunt in groups to avoid risking their own lives or returning home without meat. In our modern world, we do not engage in group hunting. Instead, we exhibit strong group behavioral tendencies because of the psychological value placed on group membership. Human beings belong to thousands of groups, from clubs, and athletic teams; from secret societies to special interest groups; including spontaneous group activities needed to respond to danger and social activities like card games and potluck meals. In each case, loyalty reflects joy and purpose in group membership and opposition to other groups when rivalry comes into play.

Authority

Authority is characterized by respect for and participation in a social hierarchy. This refers to a type of control-based authority, not power-based authority. Like the other traits, authority is an ancient foundation that comes from the survival benefits of having a leader manage a group of individuals. The benefits of a social hierarchy include accomplishing tasks that cannot be done by an individual. Research has shown that only one in ten human beings can be a leader, so when the right person is in that role, the group benefits because the leader manages members in a way that promotes efficiency. Those who are not leaders are group-oriented, comfortable being led, and happy to contribute. The authority attribute has been fundamental to the development of all societies and governments because control requires hierarchy. Those willing to respect the hierarchy receive the protection of the controlling organization. For example, if I live in a city because there is a police force to protect me, I must put up with the good and bad of city life. If I live in the country, I enjoy a better environment, but with a lower degree of safety.

Sanctity

Haidt's fifth foundation, sanctity, evolved from the human sense of disgust, which, in his early existence, helped identify danger. As omnivores, a flexible eating palate evolved to include both meat and vegetables. At birth, humans do not know what foods to eat, unlike the newborn Koala Bear who knows to eat Eucalyptus leaves. Humans have to learn what to eat and if we're good at it, we'll avoid being poisoned and increase the chances of our survival. Sanctity, in this case, means safety in knowing what food is safe to eat. Another aspect of this foundation is knowing to avoid other humans who are sick or otherwise compromised. The proximity of living in a group creates an infection or contamination risk, so avoiding the sick protects life.

Over time, sanctity has become less about shared perception of physical risk, and more about embracing a sacred belief system. The human brain has always tried to understand its world, and assign control of unexplainable events to the gods or nature. Religion was built around concepts and objects that followers venerate, so a shared philosophy tightens the group as a unit and makes it stronger.

Liberty

The final foundation principle in Haidt's list is liberty, which reflects freedom from oppression by a group. In ancient human society, before weapons, the alpha male had physical control over other males. He could exert control through his behavior and with allies, keep rivals under control. The advent of weaponry changed the rules and gave anyone who could throw a spear the ability to kill the alpha male. This change forced the development of adaptive behaviors that reduced oppression and increased accommodation. As Haidt has described, fairness and liberty can be at odds with each other. For example, if we assert that being fair means we should give money to the poor, does that mean government should threaten our liberty by confiscating our assets for that purpose?

After identifying the moral foundations of human behavior, Haidt measured the strength of people's moral beliefs to see how they mapped against political affiliation. The results of those tests are stunning.

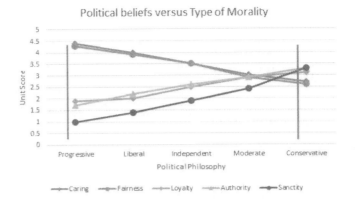

Political beliefs versus Type of Morality

Each line in the graph above represents a single moral foundation and the value placed on it by those with different political philosophies. The higher the unit number, the stronger the foundation. One can observe that the distribution of foundations in Progressives is different from that of Conservatives. Progressives highly rate caring and fairness, but the other foundations are less important to them. Conservatives rate all five foundations similarly.

Besides the obvious conclusion that Progressives and Conservatives think differently, you can see that the Conservative's morality is more complicated. Conservatives have to balance all five foundations in a way that works for them. That suggests that Conservatives may encounter difficultly making moral decisions because the choices are often not black or white. The narrowness of the Progressive morality makes them passionate about what they believe. The complexity of the Conservative morality is problematic because there can be many conflicts between the foundations. Perhaps Conservatives gravitate toward the status quo because their complicated morality often leaves them uneasy.

Haidt's conclusions led him to more completely describe the differences between WEIRD and non-WEIRD people. The WEIRDs look at the world in an analytical fashion and disconnect people from their context; they then assign them to a category and assume what is true of the category is true for the individual. Their moral systems are individualistic, rule-based, and Universalist. In other words, the WEIRDs are Progressives. As Haidt says, their morality is designed to govern a society of autonomous individuals by focusing on categories, not individuals. Categories like women, African-Americans, gays, or union workers are examples of groups the Progressives would support or want to help.

The non-WEIRDS see society as made up of relationships, contexts, groups, and institutions, with much less focus on the individual. Here, loyalty matters, authority matters, and liberty matters, adding up to a more complex moral outlook. If you have loyalty and respect for the authority of the system you belong to, then you don't want it to change. You are Conservative in that respect. For many Conservative people, the Constitution was designed to protect the liberty of the individual, so it is consistent with what they believe. When non-WEIRDS face intergroup conflicts, they employ the liberty foundation to balance the group's control of the individual. Loyalty is earned when liberty is available in the correct proportion.

In addition to individual moral beliefs, Haidt explored group behavior to see if it has a genetic component similar to individual behavior. Darwin originally suggested that natural selection was partly group-driven, meaning characteristics of a group could give it advantages over other groups. Haidt found four examples supporting Darwin.

- Kinship

- Shared intentionality

- Group evolution

- Speed of natural selection

The first case is the kinship between human group behavior and other ultra-social societies. For example, throughout history, humans were exposed to the same threats as societies of wasps: protecting the cave (nest); having offspring with an extended period of dependency before adulthood; and dealing with conflict with other groups. Mesopotamia was an excellent example of this phenomenon. The cities of Sumer were close together, had nearly identical economies, and used irrigation of the great rivers to support agriculture. The cities' proximity eventually led to conflict once the free land was exhausted and increased group size began exerting pressure on food resources. The result was the creation of armies and war as each city evolved a group behavior to protect itself.

Haidt's second case is shared intentionality. That behavior consists of two or more humans acting together for a purpose. One pulls down a branch while the other grabs the fruit. No other animals exhibit this behavior, and it is obviously an example of group-driven natural selection. Somewhere along the line, a few individuals developed this behavior and it caught on because it had a positive impact on survival. Along the way, this behavior must have accelerated the development of communication and language because shared interest requires agreement on an activity and the shared benefits of the outcome.

Haidt's third assertion is that the evolution of individuals and groups occurs in parallel. His primary example of this is the lactose intolerance gene. Before humans domesticated farm animals, all human beings were lactose intolerant. There was no need to drink milk after a child was weaned, so there was no need to tolerate lactose-laden milk. Once cows were used for milk production however, the lactose intolerance gene was modified, and humans started to become lactose tolerant. Today, 40% of the human population can drink milk without a reaction. Animal husbandry was a cultural development. Lactose tolerance was a genetic modification. The cultural behavior influenced the genetics in some way and influenced the entire group.

The fourth example supporting group selection is the speed of the natural selection process. There is evidence that gene modification has accelerated over the last 50,000 years, which may be linked to the rapid cultural evolution that has occurred during that time. The Russian scientist Belyaev (1917-1985) showed this using a novel experiment. He took wild foxes and bred them for tameness. In other words, he selected animals with the least fear of humans, and had them reproduce. Within nine generations, the foxes had become tamer and developed traits that were more akin to domesticated dogs than foxes. After thirty generations, the foxes were docile and could be used as pets.

These data suggest there is an evolved genetic group behavior that can compete against the selfishness of the individual selection process. Haidt stated it succinctly by labelling humans as "90% chimp and 10% bee." The chimp part is our natural desire to be selfish. The bee part can overcome the chimp part and bring us together under the right circumstances. We get to the bee part by turning on a "hive switch" in response to external stimuli. An obvious example of this behavior occurred in response to the 9/11 terrorist acts. Every American's hive switch flipped on and we all came together as a people within an hour of the attacks. Hundreds, if not thousands of first responders dropped what they were doing and headed for New York and Washington; donations flooded in from around the country; and we had an instant collective will to find and punish the perpetrators.

How does the human brain process its moral views? Haidt believes that the mind is a combination of controlled and automatic processes and the automatic, or intuitive, processes are in control. In situations where humans have mixed feelings, they rely on intuitive judgements as truth and look for reasons to back them up. No doubt, this derives from ages spent living in the wild where fast decision-making was the key to survival. Moral beliefs are not developed by the individual, for the individual, but rather to outfit the individual to interact with other humans. Morality is essentially a human-built set of rules that allow man to operate successfully in a group.

The Meaning of Genetic Moral Behaviors

The fact that there are genetic moral behaviors means we need to consider how they impact man in society. If morality is relative, and government is based on a collective morality, then stakeholders in government must be willing to negotiate a moral middle ground, instead of rigidly holding to extreme positions.

Individual morality is the driver for our political ideology. Those on the Left are caring and fairness driven. They support big government as the agency to provide for the poor and the disadvantaged. Those on the Right care, but not as much because their beliefs are more complex and require balance with other moral foundations. What is important is that any political system must achieve a balance between or among ideologies to move forward. Ideally, to benefit the Right and the Left, our government must balance the variations in ideologies. When the scale is unbalanced, as it is today, we see danger in the acts of the legislature because they exclude the views of the other side and do not achieve the goal of governing all the people.

The Progressive Gene

The title of this book, "progressive gene" refers to the genetic predisposition toward the belief system of the political Left, the Progressives' side of the political spectrum. The term applies because Progressives have specific observable characteristics: a narrow set of moral foundations causing an outsized focus on caring and fairness; a Utopian point of view; a strong dependence on science; and an idealistic belief that government is the change agent.

Because Progressives have a narrow set of foundations, they do not have the moral balance of those on the Right. It is not a question of whether Conservatives have better morals and are more righteous than Progressives. The issue is, those on the Right, because of their broader moral foundation set, must reconcile morality in a way Progressives do not. That distinction leads to the Right's more balanced position on political issues. Regarding economic equality, for example, Progressives see that issue solely from a caring/fairness standpoint. To them, inequality produces poverty, which is unfair to the poor, so their fairness and care foundations empathize with the suffering and they want to alleviate it. Conservatives focus more on how to fix the poverty problem, as opposed to discussing how it began. They would like to help but only if the method of helping doesn't violate their other moral foundations. For example, if wealth redistribution compromises the Right's liberty, then doesn't that make the case that redistribution is wrong?

The Progressive Gene is the innate moral philosophy of the political Left, as identified by Haidt. His research and findings have shown that morality is relative, based on a genetic disposition, and on the cultural influence of the society where the individual lives. His conclusions debunk the notion of absolute morality and tear down two thousand years of philosophical debate.

CHAPTER THREE

HUMAN EVOLUTION AND MORALITY

*Human beings will be happier - not when they cure cancer
or get to Mars or eliminate racial prejudice or flush Lake
Erie but when they find ways to inhabit primitive
communities again. That's my utopia.*

Kurt Vonnegut

Human evolutionary origins are clearly established, and we
know the first organisms on earth emerged billions of years
ago. Over those eons, the wondrously complex human life
form survived. Man knew how to adapt to and submit to,
his changing environment. Our inherited intelligence
allows us to survive, learn and understand daily life and its
long-term consequences

The intelligence we possess is forever linked both to the
past and to our future by evolutionary traits. Furthermore,
we are social animals, living and working with other human
beings, sometimes amicably, sometimes antagonistically.
Regardless, our evolved human behavior demands that a
highly specialized social "morality" operates so groups can
function efficiently.

We have understood the forms and functions of our
physical selves for a long time; but our psychosocial and
moral traits have remained obscure until recently. For

example, we now know human intelligence, sociability; morality and spirituality are clearly interrelated and are genetic components within our behavior and physiological processes. What we regard as the "self," includes genetic, physiological, psychological, behavioral and spiritual traits that work together throughout our lives.

In his book, *Human: The Science Behind What Makes Us Unique* (2009), neurobiologist Michael Gazzaniga and his peers have unmasked much of the mystery surrounding our brain functions and how the brain controls our unique human behavior. His research is a useful starting point because he provides a comprehensive description of the influence our brains have over us.

Evolution and Man

Man has become the dominant species on our planet because of his superior brain, which is four or five times larger than one would expect for a mammal our size. Beyond the size advantage, there are important functional differences between humans and the rest of the animal kingdom. For example, the human brain has a highly developed prefrontal cortex that is associated with highly complex planning and thinking. In contrast to other mammals, the larger proportion of white matter in the human cortex creates the capacity for increased connectivity and greater reasoning ability. While other mammals have a bilateral prefrontal cortex, we have a third prefrontal area that is the seat of rational decision-making. It is not the anatomical differences between us and other mammals and primates that matters, it is the capacity for intelligence that allows us to have dominion over the rest of the animal kingdom.

After a split off the evolutionary branch that contained the ancestor of humans and chimpanzees, early hominids abandoned the jungle for the grasslands of the savannah. They evolved to walk upright, giving up the opposed big toe to gain better support while standing. Their pelvises shrank to facilitate walking and thumbs developed a flexibility that made hands more useful for holding objects. Walking upright facilitated speech because a bipedal animal does not have to keep its lungs inflated to counteract the pounding of walking on all fours. These evolutionary changes in dexterity and mobility were accompanied by increases in brain size. The brain grew, and as it did, our intelligence grew with it.

During the time pre-human anatomy was changing, hominid thinking became more sophisticated. Man developed a theory of mind (TOM) which is unique in the animal kingdom. TOM refers to ability to understand life outside one's own existence, to know that others have minds like ours and, through observation and communication, to understand what others are thinking. TOM develops in children around age four or five, later becoming critical to our ability to operate in a group. It functions by shortcutting the process of understanding the behavior of others, saving the time required to understand that behavior through other types of communication. It also helps with friend or foe recognition, although it can make mistakes.

Speech has a more critical role in human behavior and is unique among animals. The anatomy of the human larynx has evolved to support the use of breaths to make sounds. At some point in man's history, this ability became a survival advantage so speaking developed as a method of controlling and influencing others. Speaking is the faster and more reliable way to find out what another person is thinking or is about to do. Here again, there is a price to pay. Since the human throat is designed to combine breathing with swallowing, we face a choke risk every time we eat.

Humans and chimps, as close cousins, share the tendency for violence, a characteristic of their group behavior. Richard Wrangham, Professor of Biology at Harvard stated, "Only two animal species are known to behave with a system of intense, male initiated territorial aggression including lethal raiding into neighboring communities in search of vulnerable enemies to attack and kill."[2] Only two animal species on earth kill their own kind: humans and chimpanzees.

At some point in history, our ancestors gained a survival advantage by killing other humans and that advantage became a component of human personality. The capability and motivation to kill is not strong in all people. Some find it easy to kill; other cannot do it. Research suggests that pride is the psychological component that pushes man to kill. Proof of that appears every time we turn on the news and hear about a domestic shooting. Evolutionary psychologists tell us the drive to kill may be driven by a secondary goal of increasing status, or possibly "homicide adaption," which comes into play when the rewards are high and the risks are low.

Social psychologists have stated that group loyalty and hostility follow from the desire for pride of status. Members of a group look at other groups as adversaries and seek to replace them in status by adopting "us versus them" behaviors. Groups also have their own internal dynamics that require members to compete for leadership.

The Social Man

Human beings live in communities because, by nature, they are social creatures. Since the driver for adaptation in nature is superiority in procreation, man has adapted his social skills to create a sexual advantage. This advantage gets him power, control, and protection. Over time, humans developed two types of social interaction: meaningful ones (family) and manipulative ones (gaining advantage by influencing others). Meaningful relationships protect the family and create a kinship unit to care for and protect offspring to improve their chances of survival. Manipulative relationships protect the interests of the family by expanding the ring of protection and gaining an understanding of forces that may threaten it.

Researchers suggest that social development and mental capacity are related; they are linked together because predicting and manipulating the behavior of others offered our species a survival advantage that offset the cost of competition. Then, as time passed, the increasing complexity of our social behavior pushed forward the development of the human brain. Our brain continued to evolve in complexity and function to meet the needs of the social human until, at some point, further development became too expensive a metabolic process to continue.

Human social groups are limited in size to about one hundred. Why? It probably correlates with the brain's ability to keep track of detailed information about members of the group. It is a lot easier to remember one hundred faces than a thousand, but social interaction is more than remembering faces. Individuals must communicate frequently and spend time with other humans in order to manipulate them. In this case, group size has a practical limit based on the number of complex interactions that can take place between people.

Gossip is another fundamental social behavior, and is essentially an evolved mechanism designed to establish truth -- to validate beliefs by seeking the input of others. If we ask a trustworthy friend to validate some fact, we can rely on what he tells us. If we seek information from strangers, there must be ways to establish the truth about what they tell us. Human beings commonly use gossip to test others for trustworthiness, and it can be a lifesaver when the consequences of misplaced trust include murder.

The degree of social skill required for mating is another factor correlated with brain size. In fact, flirting has helped make our brains larger. Flirting is an advanced communication technique with one purpose, attracting the opposite sex. At stake is the proliferation of our gene pool, so elegant speech and persuasive arguments need to be designed to attract attention from the opposite sex. The number of words necessary for life's normal activities is small so there is no evolutionary reason why man needed a complex vocabulary to survive. We developed that vocabulary to influence others, particularly the opposite sex.

Deception sits on the risky side of social behavior. Some people intentionally deceive and communicate untruths to gain advantage. Sometimes it works, such as when victims are unfamiliar with the deceiver. Most of the time it does not because humans have a built in "cheater detection" system that can tell if people are lying. We can recognize intentional deception separate from the unintentional kind, so we do not penalize someone for making a mistake. Habitual cheaters are eventually isolated from the group when knowledge of their behavior spreads and they are caught. Our memories are stronger for cheaters than honest people.

The Moral Man

The last topic in our journey through human behavior is morality, which is the set of rules humans live by to facilitate compatibility with others in human society. Morality is an evolved behavior resulting from man's adaptation to his social environment. The fact that ninety-five percent of us get along shows how well human beings have adapted to living in large groups. That adaptation requires a trade-off: subverting selfish desires in exchange for acceptance and benefits enjoyed by group membership. Some morals are universal, such as "thou shalt not kill." Other less significant rules may be adapted to the individual and their group. Without morality, people would repeatedly commit acts only to benefit themselves, cause harm to others, and destabilize social groups.

Researchers have shown that human decision-making contains an emotional and a rational component. Individuals with damage to the emotional centers of their brains have difficulty making decisions. A similar phenomenon occurs in psychopaths who lack empathy because of damage to those centers; they have no brakes to prevent them from violent acts toward others.

Our decision-making mechanism involves rational thought processes that are secondary to emotional responses, so when a set of options is presented, a stored emotion is applied. If that emotion is negative toward one option (I didn't like that flavor of ice cream last time), then the option is discarded. After the options evoking negative emotions are eliminated, the rational thought process begins. (Last time I was with someone I'd just met, and I was nervous. Now, I'm alone and would like to order that flavor again.)

It's easy to understand why we make decisions this way. For most of our history, human lives have been under threat and the responses to those threats needed to be either intuitive ones (based on biological response) or emotional ones (from previous experiences). Primitive man, hunting on the savannah and encountering a lion, did not have time to apply logic to his decision process.

Humans use two types of decision-making processes: intentional and preconscious. We make intentional decisions a thousand times a day: what to wear, what to eat, does my car need gas, etc. Pre-conscious decision making (also called affective priming) is a continuous set of reactions and responses we feel toward our environment. As we move through the world, our senses are gathering information (smells, visual, noises) that are processed against a set of stored attitudes in our minds. For example, you walk into a room with an ugly carpet (at least you think it is ugly) and you have a reaction. The decision process takes place instantly without your awareness. You gather your perceptions; compare them to stored attitudes and, a microsecond later, you think "Ugh!"

Preconscious decision-making developed as a defense mechanism. Those who made the fewest errors identifying a dangerous situation survived. By necessity, this preconscious processing has a strong negative bias, because we need to remember dangerous situations more strongly than beneficial ones. Negative responses raise our blood pressure and heart rate because our primitive brains put the rest of our brain on high alert: we may have to flee, fight, or freeze to protect ourselves and others. For example, when you examine a meal put in front of you at a restaurant, sensory information allows your brain to analyze the food and look for danger. It ignores the fact that the beans look good and concentrates on the fact that the meat smells bad, like the way it smelled the time it made you sick.

There are two types of moral judgements in human behavior: personal and impersonal. Personal moral judgments reflect a protective mechanism for the good of the family. Humans find it more difficult to harm a friend than a stranger, if the choice arises. This makes sense from an evolutionary standpoint; if we protect our clan, we protect our genes. Interpersonal moral decision-making judgments do not elicit an emotional response; those judgements are based on conscious thinking about the situation. In the case of the famous "trolley dilemma," a test subject decides whether or not to divert a trolley so it kills only one person to save the lives of five others. We make decisions like this based on the greater good being more important than preventing harm to the few.

Beyond behavioral adaptation, our morality is derived from a genetic component; that is an innate set of what scientists call "moral modules" that help guide us through the decision-making process. These modules contribute to decision-making in the absence of other data and their existence relates to categories of decision-making that were required in our hunter-gatherer history. The process of making moral judgments starts with a stimulus which leads to a positive or negative response and produces an emotional state in the individual. That emotional state calls on stored moral responses applicable to the current situation. Because there are multiple moral modules, two or more of them may compete for control over the pending decision. For example, a moral concept of liberty could compete with a moral concept of authority when one feels oppressed by decisions made by a leader with influence over him. These moral modules of caring, fairness, loyalty, authority, sanctity, and liberty were identified by Jonathan Haidt and discussed in the previous chapter.

Individual morality does not give us license to behave badly, because the morality of society places limits on what we're allowed to do. The community expresses an evolving set of standards (laws, mores) and expects its members to abide by them. This group morality evolves as a reaction to forces that may harm the group's effectiveness, so it is always working toward creating institutional consensus.

Man's moral foundations are a part of his physical being, such as height, weight, personality, and the desire to live in a group. Morality is fundamental to our behavior and exerts influence over every action we take. Because it is genetic and adapted to a final form in childhood, morality is not easily altered in adulthood. We tend to react and respond in the same way to similar situations. Morality is also relative, as seen in the variation of political views in contemporary America. The morality of a society is the full tally of the individuals who are part of it, operating as an external entity. The health of any culture depends on a moral consensus, because without that, the culture cannot maintain stability.

CHAPTER FOUR

MAN BUILDS A CULTURE

*In ancient times the ritual, mythological and doctrinal
aspects of spiritual space were predominant.*

Tom Turner

Ancient political systems developed out of the conditions
and needs of those whose benefits were at stake. As they
evolved into socio-political beings, people's essential needs
extended beyond food, clothing and shelter, to agricultural
control, surplus, trade, protection from outsiders, peace,
prosperity and order. Having a voice in socio-political life
and decisions was a key survival tool; oppression, tyranny
or dictatorship did not foster human development or
progress.

The greatest challenge of man was (and is) the building of
societies -- the social structure where human beings live
together in large groups. The need for societies was a direct
result of the radical increase in family, clan, tribe, and
diverse group sizes that emerged with the advent of
agriculture. Once humans learned to produce food in high
volume, they settled in fruitful places and cities evolved to
support large numbers of people. Cities placed new
demands on social behavior, because people were forced to
interact with large numbers of strangers. The customs of

family and clan were not useful, so new behaviors had to evolve.

As the first cities developed, a natural division of labor appeared, separating men by attitude and aptitude. Those with wealth of some kind (property or money) exerted control, while others chose to run their own businesses, work for a business owner, or work as laborers. Professional skills developed, such as auditor or legal expert, and a division of labor in farming emerged. Farmers needed a method to get their products to market, so they worked to develop distribution systems utilizing shippers, wholesalers, and retailers.

Companion to division of labor was a social class stratum. In the beginning, it was as simple as separating those who would comply with the rules from those who wouldn't. Eventually, social classes became more differentiated based on economic status, profession, or educational level.

The final piece of this new human structure was government, which was built out of the necessity for centralized authority. Government's first role was to provide safety and protection but then, gradually, it took over management of the economy. In man's egalitarian days, links between groups were fluid and without boundaries, the opposite of the structure required for government. In human organization, equality and authority were, and are, incompatible. Authority implies a hierarchy, and pure equality will not allow it.

Culture contains a morality held in common by those who are members of that culture. It has many characteristics, so there must be individuals who are "keepers" of a culture, or promulgators, along with individuals who are "enforcers" and arbitrators of a culture. A culture is successful when it allows its members to co-exist in harmony while adapting to changing economic, social, and political conditions. A culture is threatened when it is unable to return to equilibrium after stress. Historically, cultures have failed because their leaders were unable to adapt, adopt, or overcome factors that created instability. Just like humans as biological machines, culture, as a social machine, ages and eventually dies, giving way to a new socio-political and cultural arrangement.

Each culture has a unique morality associated with it. That morality is a mixture of the moralities of its citizens influenced by their environment, so changes to either or both will impact the culture's morality. Environmental changes include wars, natural disasters, and economic distress. Changes to the citizenry occur in periods of immigration when other people come in from the outside. The impact of immigration is uncertain, until it reaches a point of massive disruption. The disruption is directly related to the number of people coming in and the affinity between the existing culture and the incoming culture. Major differences mean longer assimilation and greater disruption.

The Mesopotamian Culture

Man began his march toward complex societies during the Neolithic Age, which began about 10,000 BC. By the end of this period, around 3,000 BC, he was farming, raising domesticated animals, and making tools out of bronze. The Neolithic Age began in the Levant, an area of the eastern Mediterranean between Turkey and Egypt, now consisting of Israel, Lebanon, Syria, Jordan, Cyprus, part of southern Turkey, and Iraq. Archaeology of the region provides the first evidence of agricultural activity on earth. Farmers cultivated rye, and through records and artifacts, we have evidence that the human consumption of wild cereals took place during the initial period. Human dwellings were made of wood and set over a dry, stone foundation with a diameter that was typically nine to eighteen feet around a central fireplace. Settlements included about one hundred and fifty people. Tools were widely used; sickles appeared for the first time along with knives, arrowheads, and stone bowl mortars. Domesticated dogs were present, and the dead were buried in caves or covered with stones.

The nucleus of human development in the Levant was Mesopotamia. The name is a Greek word meaning, "between the rivers," which references the great Tigris and Euphrates. In the northern section, the rivers were close together and the land between them was hilly and watered by the many nearby tributaries. In the southern part, where the rivers were separate by as much as one hundred miles, the first civilization of man appeared.

This was the home of Sumer and Akkad, later called Babylonia. Rainfall is rare in this region, but storms appear suddenly. The sun beats down and winds produce dust storms. Left to nature, this geography would consist of mud flats, stagnant pools and reed swamps. No building materials or metals had been found there, but there was soil to offset all that was missing. It was easily worked and there was an endless supply of water. Farmers in that area expanded their numbers enormously and created an agricultural output that, when combined with the other things needed by man, produced a civilization. Building that civilization was delayed until man had mastered the techniques of irrigation. Without that technology, the natural ebb and flow of the rivers left a salt residue, which ruined the soil for plants.

Initial developments were not located near the rivers, but farther north where the Mesopotamian lowlands and the

Zagros Mountains of Kurdistan collide. This is the region referred to as the Assyrian Steppe. Here, the land had sufficient rainfall for dry farming but also access to areas where hunting and gathering wild food were possible. Mixed food production dominated until about 4,000 BC, when tribes mastered irrigation techniques and drifted southward toward the alluvial plain. As irrigation techniques improved, and food production increased, southern urban centers grew exponentially. The rivers became an enormous economic boon. Their soft earth eased the task of cultivation; they provided unlimited water for crop irrigation; and they were a ready means of transportation to and from locations that could supply raw materials, and foodstuffs, including marine life.

The First Urban Environment

How did Mesopotamia evolve into an urban environment? As the anthropologist, Elman Service (1915-1996), has described, there is a logical progression of human organization from egalitarian to chiefdom, to pre-government, to classical government. A chiefdom has a centralized direction, hereditary hierarchical arrangements, some basic aristocracy, but no formal legal system for forceful repression. This structure is almost universally theocratic and loyalty flows from the congregation to the priest. A pre-government stage follows as soon a society passes through the chiefdom phase, and acquires defining characteristics. The first of these characteristics is a voluntary hierarchy where people come under the influence of a leader who can offer them safety and sustenance in return for loyalty.

Second, there is a landholding regime where agricultural workers are tied to the land as serfs. Third, there is an economic system of near self-sufficiency that results from the efforts of the hierarchy.

The period between 3,500 and 3,000 BC in Mesopotamian history is labeled the Fluorescent Period because of rapid growth and diversification of its cities. One of these, Warka, contained a temple that took 7500-man-years to build. It contained housing for priests and their staff, providing evidence of a religious chiefdom. By 3,000 BC, there were about twenty cities in Sumer and they were thriving. It was then that writing began. In a theocracy, the most important structure in the city was the temple, which served as a house of worship and grain storage facility. Archaeologists have uncovered artifacts and sites that include evidence of a great deal of craft specialization and show sophisticated techniques and artistry.

Other advances during the Fluorescent Period included the manufacture of mechanical devices such as plows, wheeled carts, and rafts with sails. By that time, the water of the great rivers was controlled and managed by canals and channels designed to cover each city's farmlands. Like the canals, roads were laid out in geometric patterns. Farmers used wooden plows, seed drills, and stone hoes to work their barley. Shepherds and dogs watched over flocks of sheep; gardens containing fruit trees were walled; and date palms overshadowed the terrain. Donkeys on roads and boats on the canals carried the harvest to the cities, and they were surrounded by sun-dried mud walls and moats. The walls around Uruk, a typical site, stretched some six miles and contained nine hundred towers.

Within the gates of the cities, armed soldiers watched traffic consisting of chariots and wagons traveling by the homes of the wealthy. Behind the mansions were the modest huts of the farmers, who arose and left them for the fields each day. Small shops were ubiquitous: potters, smiths, and other artisans worked and plied their trade.

Along with socio-economic and cultural development came political and religious revolutions. While the first villages were masses of undifferentiated workers tightly grouped by their own economic and spiritual unity, economic classes emerged later. At the top were the priests who evolved over time into messengers for the gods and supervisors of temple land holdings. Half of those holdings were rented to peasants who paid with one-third to one-sixth of their crops in rent. They were paid in silver when selling their crops at the market. Untilled land was cultivated by peasants organized in guilds under foremen. The priests also controlled large flocks, watercraft, fishermen, brewers, bakers, and spinners of wool. Raw materials were brought in by merchants who used the waterways to trade in stone, metals, wood, and jewels. The priests held the states together, although their position and that of kings, who appeared later, pushed the citizenry into dependency.

After a time, interstate warfare commenced, leading to forms of imperialism which then drove the evolution of military classes. Bureaucracies were developed to manage the larger cities. Slavery also appeared during this time as citizens who could not pay their debts, or those unfortunate enough to be captured in war, became the chattel of the wealthy and victorious. Slaves were not used in agriculture but lived in cities and worked as merchants or artisans.

Class stratification was social, not economic and it shaped the political state. Social stratification resulted from the variations in human behavior within a group, between groups, and among groups. Some members, through personality, physical strength, or motivation, rose to positions of respect and authority over others; individuals' lack of intelligence, misbehavior, or social incompatibility came to be disrespected by the higher groups and those unfortunates fell to the lowest status levels.

In Mesopotamia, social stratification and the differentiation of labor led to socio-economic stratification and then a political system. The wealthy sought to control the masses while the masses agitated through their sheer numbers for the rights they felt they deserved. The most important social trend of the time saw tribal farmers falling into peasantry under the economic demands of the state. Here, as in countless times throughout history, the social pattern had one division, splitting an upper and lower class. The upper class began to develop forms of exploitation and assumed a cultural superiority.

Transition to Monarchy

As the Mesopotamian culture matured, it made the transition from a religion-based authoritarian structure to a dynastic phase, assuming the characteristics of a monarchy. The twenty cities of the alluvial plain urbanized as they concentrated themselves defensively. Aggression arose when the last free land was taken and pressures to feed a growing urban populace were exerted from the inside. As war became chronic, authoritarian governments came into being and were the means for building, equipping and utilizing an army. The warfare during this period was of two types: against neighbors; and against nomadic tribes in the northern territories.

In the first case, the cities were close enough together to make alliances valuable and war resulted when disputes could not be settled. Control of the defeated enemy was not possible because no single city was strong enough to hold external territory.

The other kind of war, pitting nomadic tribes against pastoralists, was particularly difficult to wage. The nomads were mobile and the pastoralists and cities were not. One imagines that "buying off" the nomads could have been a short-term strategy for appeasement, but it is more likely that buffer zones were created to protect the cities. In Mesopotamia, during the dynastic period, military considerations influenced not only the size of a population but its location and movements.

In 2,370 BC, the Akkadian Empire was founded by Sargon, a successful military leader who united the irrigation culture of the south with the pastoral land of the north. Sargon invented a new role for himself, unlike any that had come before. He placed himself next to the gods and accordingly, required a sworn oath to him be included on every official document. Sargon's approach to governance set him apart from the public and elevated him above all others. His signature was a guarantee to those participating in a transaction; an assurance they would receive the protection of his government. The empire of Sargon lasted four generations before it was overrun by the Guti tribe.

The reign of Sargon was important for the development of political systems because his reign transitioned the Mesopotamian culture into a new form. Two principles of statecraft were in operation; borrow the best components from another culture to improve on the older one; adapt the borrowed components until they are compatible with their new surroundings. Compatibility must develop, or the new culture cannot thrive. An example of these principles is found in the cities of Sumer. They were close to each other and influenced each other within their common culture. Common culture was the basis for small adaptations each city needed to make. This dynamic cultural change was like having twenty entrepreneurs in the same neighborhood, developing a similar product and sharing their acquired knowledge. In the case of Sumer's cities, the end- product was a working urban culture.

The Mesopotamian world provided important contributions to the future of governments. Its political trend was toward territories larger than any that had come before. The pace of growth allowed the political, bureaucratic, and military systems to develop slowly. Writing and mathematics moved forward, alongside statecraft. Cultural components such as economics, law, and religion developed according to political demands.

Mesopotamia stands as the world's first true urban civilization, but understanding its growth presents some challenges because of the lack of sufficient historical detail. Facts tell us that repeated warfare internally and externally, along with the development of agriculture and animal domestication, had an enormous impact on the growth of its cities. That growth required a new political system, so the theocracy fell away and was replaced by the more efficient monarchy. Monarchical forms would become the standard political system in the western world for more than four thousand years.

CHAPTER FIVE

MAN CREATES POLITICAL SYSTEMS

The center of Western culture is Greece, and we have never lost our ties with the architectural concepts of that ancient civilization.

Stephen Gardiner

The models for our modern government were created by the ancient Greeks, who developed the first democracies, and by the Romans who built the first Republic. The Greeks preceded the Romans because they were closer to other developing cultures in the Fertile Crescent; had access to the sea, which fostered communications with the outside world; and possessed a unique geography. Greek democracy, called the Polis, emerged in the 8th Century BC, following the Greek Dark Ages, and lasted until Greece fell to Macedonia in the mid-fourth Century BC. Etruscan kings ruled Rome in the mid-8th Century BC but the Romans expelled that monarchy in 509 BC and created a Republic, which lasted until its transition to an autocratic political system starting in 30 BC.

The Greek and Roman political systems were separated from what came before them because they took significant steps forward for individual rights. As discussed in the last chapter, the governments that came before them were theocracies, based on a chiefdom structure or hereditary monarchies. The latter, originating with Sargon, flowed in a continuous line down to the time of the Greeks through the Minoan and the Mycenaean Civilizations.

The Greeks paved the way for individual rights by promoting independent thinking (philosophy), and that led to a new set of ideas about how best to govern people. Instead of ruling through strength and leadership, the men of Athens showed how ideas could push their culture forward. To the Greeks, the human mind sought independence based on the principles of justice and fairness. Over the centuries of Greek development, mathematics, science, philosophy, drama, and medicine advanced in ways man could not have imagined previously.

Evolution of the Polis

The idea of the Polis evolved from circumstances that supported a break from the monarchies. Around 750 BC, Greek development began when an aristocratic class came to power as the controlling faction of Greek society. As they acquired wealth, the aristocrats asserted their independence as individuals. They began to create social distinctions to separate themselves from the commoners and adopted a more refined and cultured way of life. That, in turn, fostered a more conscious focus on man's nature and place. External influence was strong and the aristocrats did not limit themselves in any way, demanding new models for artistic expression.

Early on, the upper classes realized the value of passing on their cultural model to succeeding generations. Fathers set standards for their children's education and hired tutors and philosophers to teach them. As the children grew, peer pressure compelled them to conform to their class, so there was a tightening of the model. The aristocracy expanded but not without constraints. Their class could not discard its own history, where kinship links to the rest of society, preventing class separation. The masses, despite lacking political power, possessed unity in numbers and skills essential to the aristocracy. In the end, the delicate balance between the classes was protected by geographical isolation, so Greece was free to incubate its city-state in a pure form without interference from the outside.

The structure of the Polis required a defined geographical unit, organized locally as a concentrated set of urban dwellings. With the emergence of the city-state, military, religious and political functions were in one place. Courts became centrally located and geographically separated religious functions were brought together in the temple of the state gods. The most important Poleis (cities) became economic centers, attracting potters and other artisans to re-locate there. Their initial growth was not a result of commercial activity, but rather, the complex organization of an agrarian society. Athens, in the beginning, was a group of villages located around the fortress Acropolis. Because the connection between government and people was a loose one, there were no walls until hundreds of years later when the people had money to build them. The people, not the structures are what mattered. As Alcaeus said, "Neither houses, finely roofed, or canals and dockyards make the city, but men able to use their opportunity."

The aristocrats gained the most from the emerging political system by consolidating their power. They became the officers of the state and imposed their moral and artistic preferences on the people. That is not to say class power was out of balance, because the Polis was fundamentally a reaction of its entire citizenry to the problems of the age. All classes were convinced they had to work together to make sure the changing world did not produce chaos. One can see, in the restriction of individual freedom for the good of the whole, a brake was applied to the aristocratic class, whether they agreed to it or not; there was a balance between the classes that would last for hundreds of years.

The Polis continued to evolve despite obstacles. Because it depended on a delicate balance between an aristocratic class and the common people, the Polis was subject to any disruption that upset that balance. Tyrants emerged over a 150-year period starting in 650 BC. Those were not tyrants as the dictionary defines them, but mostly competent autocrats who cared for their people. They appeared because there was always a tendency for the aristocracies to become more oppressive, leading to popular support for someone who could take power on their behalf. But the Greek tyrants were never able accumulate enough power to establish continuity. The Age of Tyrants ended when the Greek democracy became more stable.

Solon

A second disruption in the history of the Polis took place in Athens, starting in the early 6th Century BC. Solon, one of the dominant figures in the history of Greek politics, rose to power and played a pivotal role in the architecture of the Greek democracy. He was an educated aristocrat, successful businessman, and poet who was the right person in a time of peril. In the year 600 BC, Athenian politics were in complete disarray. The prior decades had seen the fall of the pottery trade behind the Corinthian competition, so the city was suffering economically. Meanwhile, the Athenian aristocratic class had become more ruthless. Poor farmers became serfs of the rich when they could not pay their debts, the landless were enslaved and were sold abroad.

Solon himself tells us that it was with reluctance that he took charge as an objective leader, concerned over the avarice of the rich, and the desperation of the poor. He was chosen Archon in 593 BC, to act as an arbitrator and lawgiver at once, because "the rich had confidence in him as a man of easy fortune, and the poor trusted him as a good man." (Plutarch's Lives, Volume 1, Solon). Solon chose to proceed quietly as administrator to not disturb or overset the state, because he would not have sufficient power to reconstitute and organize it again, if he failed the first time. To rule properly, Solon thought it best to "Combine force and justice together." So, he started changing existing laws, in fact, he changed nearly all of them.

Solon did not believe democracies were practical. In his mind, the only proper way to organize the state was as a republic using the distribution of wealth. Anticipating the Roman Republic, which was still ninety years in the future, he rejected equality, choosing instead to create a balance between the classes. Solon believed the creation of a middle class would neutralize the conflict between the upper and lower, which is precisely the role the Knights would play in Republican Rome. Solon's year in power ended with passions high, yet there was enough support in each class for his reforms to keep the Polis stable. He ordered the new laws to be in force for one hundred years, and then, to the surprise of many, resigned his post and left Athens. The Athenian Polis returned to a democracy, but the reforms of Solon had made it stronger.

The Golden Age of Athens

Following the wars with Persia, which ended in 479 BC, Athens entered a new age led by Pericles. He was an aristocrat, with the gifts of intelligence and leadership. He became the leader of the council of ten generals and served as the de facto ruler of Athens from 461 BC until his death in 429 BC. During his tenure, Pericles passed laws allowing poor citizens to attend plays for free, and began a system of compensation for magistrates and jurors. This allowed a broader spectrum of the populace to participate in government. He also lowered the property qualification for the archonship to help break up the monopoly of the aristocratic class. The time of Pericles, in fact and in historic parlance, was the Golden Age of Athens because the stable, open democracy provided the fuel for Athenian intellectual development.

Sadly, this period also signaled the beginning of the end for Athens. After the Persian Wars, the city became imperialistic. Leaders sought to extend their power around the Aegean to protect their city from invasion and bolster their economic interests. Athenian arrogance alienated its allies, particularly Sparta, and this led directly to the Peloponnesian War in 431 BC. Thirty years of fighting Sparta devastated and destroyed Athens and it never recovered. By the time Philip of Macedonia rose to power, a fragmented Greece could not stop him. The end for Athens came at the Battle of Chaeronea in 338 BC.

Loss of military and economic control was the larger symptom of the decay that lay beneath the surface when the cleavage between rich and poor began to have a destabilizing effect on Greek politics. The willingness of the poor to subscribe to the idealism of the Polis was worn away and their desire for equal rights was out in the open. The people wanted a re-distribution of land and a cancellation of debts. The rich, for their own part, formed oligarchic clubs as their way to maintain control. Aristotle quoted one of the club's oaths, which said, "I will be an enemy to the people, and devise all the harm against them which I can."

This is the history of the rise and fall of the Polis, one of the greatest civilizations built by man, and toppled by decay and indifference.

The Roman Republic

Greek and Roman civilizations mirrored specific influences of human character. The Greek character was idealistic and intellectual; the Roman character was quite the opposite and shaped a political structure that was practical and organized. While Greece was a mountainous peninsula, Italy had its own unique, expansive topography, so geography and human traits molded those ancient civilizations into entirely separate but successful forms.

The Roman people were a mixture of Latin and Etruscan tribes who settled in central Italy around the 9th Century BC. Their true origins are unclear; they may have come from Europe or possibly the Middle East. The city of Rome was established in the mid-7th Century BC. Folklore sets the traditional date of founding as an Etruscan kingdom in 753 BC. In 509 BC, the monarchy was overthrown and the Republic was established. Development during the early Republican period was influenced by the character of the Roman people and the political system they inherited from the Etruscans. They were an independent race, united, and possessing a strong, collective will to survive as a people. Very early, the Romans exhibited the traits that would make them successful: the desire to organize, the ability to adapt, and a sense of cultural unity. The experience of victory in war reinforced the Roman belief that they were destined for greatness. Success drove them to expand the Republic regionally, across the Italian peninsula, to the western Mediterranean, and finally to the Greek peninsula, giving them control of the Mediterranean Sea.

The Romans took the tribal government of the kings and retained most of the old structure in their Republic. The old council of elders became the Senate, the people's Assembly was retained in like form, and a new magistrate position, the consul, was substituted for the king. The resulting political system was balanced, with each branch assigned a base of authority and shared controls over it. The Senate made foreign policy and introduced new bills to the Assembly, but it could not pass laws. The Assembly could not introduce bills but was responsible for passing them. There were two consuls elected simultaneously for a one-year term of office. They acted as the primary administrators on behalf of the Senate and held veto rights over each other.

That balanced political structure was vital because it prepared Rome to meet the forces acting on it from within and outside. Internally, the plebian class was restless and demanded more rights. Externally, Rome's enemies were poised to attack and destroy her. The Roman class struggle took some two hundred and thirty years to resolve, but was accomplished peacefully because the Senate was willing to extend rights to the plebian class. At first, Rome's view of war was defensive but later evolved into a successful policy of creating colonial outposts to serve as buffers between the Republic and its enemies. Having the class struggle resolved by 287 BC removed a key distraction from Roman focus on foreign policy. That focus would be needed to fight sovereign countries and protect the borders of the Republic.

Beginning of the End

By 133 BC, the Roman Republic was at its zenith and was the most successful power in the Mediterranean. Alongside status was internal conflict from economic uncertainty and increasing poverty. A slave war in Sicily in 139 BC had interrupted grain shipments to Rome; soon there was a severe food shortage. Such shortages were most acute among the urban poor whose numbers were increasing as unsuccessful small farmers were moving to the city to find work and a better life.

When changes in land ownership occurred, qualification for the army changed with them. Historically, the Republic had operated as a society ruled by landowners, so serving in the army required a man to own property; those without property could not serve. In the early days when the population was small, the army was essentially a militia called into action to protect the lives and property of its citizens. When a war ended, soldiers went back to their farms. Rome had fought many wars during the middle period of the Republic and those conflicts had a serious impact on the ability of the government to sustain an army.

Later wars lasted longer and were fought farther from home, so farmers serving in the army became destitute while they were away because their farms were not worked and did not generate income. With the Romans fighting constantly, there was also a tremendous loss of life, and new recruits had to be obtained to replace those who had fallen. In 107 BC, the Consul Marius, relaxed the property rules for military service and proposed that the army be paid by its generals out of the spoils of war. That act destabilized the republic because it shifted the focus of the army's loyalty from the Senate to the military leader and produced the unintended consequence of making generals kingmakers. The first fifty years of the 1st Century BC saw rapid swings in power as the Senate tried to keep control, only to lose it to the army when the public perceived a power vacuum. In the end, the Senate and aristocratic class were overwhelmed by events neither could control, and the Roman Republic collapsed from the erosion of its original ideals.

Clearly visible in the Roman experience were all the classic elements driving governmental change: instability created by lack of power to govern; inefficiency created from lack of attention to significant societal needs; dissatisfaction with a broken system; and finally, opposition to change. Any society can tolerate difficulty and hardship for a time, maybe for decades, or even centuries, but its path is dependent on the psyche of its people. If the people are dissatisfied, a set of trigger events can destroy the political system.

The Greek and Roman political systems evolved a culture of rights and citizen participation that became fundamental to each culture. Laws were important as a check against abuses by the influential, along with impartial legal systems that created stability. That kind of stability made them superior to the popular but unstable monarchical systems.

CHAPTER SIX

THE AMERICAN CHARACTER

We need a revolution every 200 years, because all governments become stale and corrupt after 200 years.

Benjamin Franklin

Sixteen hundred years passed between the end of the Roman republic in 30 BC and the beginning of settlements in North America. During that interval, Rome became an empire, conquered the Western world, became Christian and collapsed by 476 AD. The barbarian Europe that survived was left to endure a thousand-year period of rebuilding human society from a primitive state: five hundred years of slow government evolution and five hundred years of mature government systems. By the 15th Century, Europe was alive again. The plagues had ended, commerce was thriving, and new markets needed to be found to exploit the emerging mercantile philosophy. A great period of exploration had begun, which would include a trip to the New World in 1492. The Republican political system was a continuing experiment, and four attempts were made to establish one between the time of Rome and the time of America: Venice in 800 AD; Iceland in 930; Florence in 1400; and Calvinist Holland in 1600.

Monarchies maintained their positions as the dominant political system in Europe, but before long, the Enlightenment would cause cracks in the old order.

During the 16th Century, French and Spanish explorers scoured the New World from Nova Scotia to Cape Horn, looking for precious metals. Spain explored vast portions of North and South America, while the French visited portions of the interior of North America and Canada. For a variety of reasons, large areas of the Atlantic coast of North America went unexplored. Some areas were thought to be too warm for fur trading and others too cool for tropical agriculture. A French settlement in Virginia in 1572 failed because of Indian attacks. The Spanish eventually settled in Florida because it was close to their Colonies in the Caribbean and South America but, for some reason, they never moved north. During that period, the English found themselves lagging in the exploration race, but the crown was financially strapped and could not finance colonization.

Eventually, Britain devised a way around their financial constraints by subcontracting colonization through issuing licenses to private individuals who would assume any risks in the hope of a return on their investment. The prime movers of this effort were a group of ambitious men called the "west country men" and it included such distinguished names as Sir Walter Raleigh and Sir Francis Drake. With the approval of the Crown, the first colonization was attempted by Sir Walter Raleigh in 1585, at Roanoke, in what would later become the North Carolina colony. The settlement was reinforced in 1586 but another trip could not be arranged until 1590. When that ship arrived, the settlement had been abandoned and the Colonists had disappeared. The lesson for British investors was that more serious efforts and better planning were required to settle that far away land. In fact, it took another fifteen years to get a permanent settlement established.

Colonization of the Atlantic coast of North America was driven by investors who received specific grants of territory from the King. Those men had a simple plan for exploiting their new holdings: crops would be planted; colonists would provide the labor; and ships would take the harvest to market. Their view was simplistic and lacked the understanding of what the impact would be upon the vast geography and on the prospects for commercial success. In the North, the Appalachian Mountains created a harsh, rocky terrain not suited for farming, while in the South the sub-tropical terrain was too hot for most temperate climate crops. In the end, the Colonies had to discover for themselves what could be grown. In areas where agriculture was not profitable, they had to look to commerce as a way of life. Geography drove the path of development and America and the Colonies quickly became regionalized: New England; Middle Atlantic, and the South. By the time America was ready to become a nation, its leaders saw themselves as regional representatives, as well as representatives for the interests of their states.

Enlightenment Thinking

The Enlightenment began in Europe in the late 17th Century. It was a cultural movement of intellectuals emphasizing reason and individualism, instead of tradition. The genesis for the movement was the advancement of science through the scientific method, along with a human desire to throw off superstition. The Enlightenment was also a reaction against the church-monarchy connection that had been in place for a thousand years. By declaring monarchies illegitimate, Enlightenment thinkers were also criticizing the Catholic Church, which sanctioned the monarchies.

During this period, the first Progressive intellectuals appeared, and they would set the stage for the social justice model that would be applied later during the Industrial Revolution. It was the philosophers who led the way, including John Locke (1632-1704), who is considered the father of English Liberalism. Soon, the first advocates of political morality would follow, namely Jeremy Bentham (1748-1832) and his follower, John Stuart Mill (1806-1873). Those men were the original Progressive thinkers, finding fault with a society that allowed so many of its citizens to be diseased and destitute. They were early warriors in the fight for social justice, but they came too early to make a difference because governments were not ready to adapt to the social changes needed.

The American Character

The character of the American people developed as its settlers found a toehold in the New World and overcame the challenges of its wilderness. Then, with establishment of a new society, Americans reacted against English exploitation, ultimately throwing off the yoke of the British Empire. When the Revolution ended, the American people launched a political system based on Enlightenment concepts and the ancient political systems of Rome and Athens.

The middle class of Colonial America was unique, compared to England, and took shape through the acquisition of the vast lands in the new territory. There was no upper class in the beginning; it did not form until the land was safe and the first cities had evolved. The large middle class included professional men; land-owner/farmers; small merchants; artisans; shopkeepers; and clerks. Those individuals worked hard for a living and aspired to a reasonable quality of life. Starting out with little, they managed to succeed and in doing so, expressed most strongly the qualities and traits we identify with the American character: ambition, energy, and hard work.

The Colonial middle class was stratified but not homogeneous and was based on a person's success at acquiring property. While the most affluent owners held property up to a thousand acres, the group below them owned perhaps one hundred acres. That group had no investments and had to borrow money to purchase land and equipment. A third group, consisting of nomad farmers, also existed and they worked the frontier and sold their property to others.

At the bottom of the socio-economic ladder were three groups: the poor, indentured servants, and slaves. The poor exist in any society, and in Colonial America they worked occasionally. They were improperly clothed for the climate and wandered from place to place. But, the poor were free, unlike the other two groups. Indentured servants were temporarily "owned" until they worked enough time to pay off their debt. Often, that debt amounted to the price of passage to the New World. Although those individuals made up the largest dependent class in the 17th Century, (40% of the Virginia population in 1625), their numbers decreased in the 1700s as they became free of debt and their positions were replaced by slaves.

Slavery began in Virginia in 1619 and grew steadily in the South as indentured servants completed their obligations. Southern farmers had trouble recruiting workers because of the harsh conditions of the wilderness, so slaves filled that void because they had no choice.

Early Governments

The thirteen Colonies that made up Colonial America were of two types: corporate and provincial, based on the original purpose for creating them. Massachusetts, Connecticut, and Rhode Island were, corporate; all the others were provincial, meaning possessions of the Crown. In Virginia, in 1619, the first legislative body in the Colonies formed; it included the well-known House of Burgesses. Leaders of the Virginia Company who owned the royal charter for Virginia drew up a "great charter" in 1618-19 to entice new settlers to the colony. Emigrants who paid their passage from Great Britain received 50 acres of land. They were promised representation through a governmental body, to be called the House of Burgesses.

This body was designed to give colonists a say in their own government including introducing bills to fund government activities. The Virginia legislature also had an "upper house" called the Governor's council, who served as advisers to the governor, who was appointed by the Crown. The first meeting of the legislature, which took place on July 30, 1619, included 22 elected members of the House of Burgesses. The Virginia legislature governed through some tough times until 1624, when the Virginia Company's charter was revoked for misbehavior and Virginia became a Crown colony. The governor and council were then selected by the King.

The Virginia legislature was the first of the "mini-republics" to operate in the Colonies. Before long, all the Colonial governments would utilize a similar structure.

That model met the definition of Republic as it had originated in Rome: there was no autocratic leader and there was an assembly representing the people. In most Colonies, the assembly had control of taxation, and this basic right was fundamental to the colonist's view of the structure of government.

The Eighteenth Century

If the 17th Century could be labeled a "Century of Hardship," the 18th Century would be described as a time of relative prosperity. The independent, hardworking settlers of the earlier times had conquered nature and built a society. The nation's population of 250,000 in 1700 was ten times larger by 1770, helped along by 400,000 white settlers who had arrived from foreign lands. Population growth accelerated through large families and a relatively healthy environment.

The engine for economic growth was trade, which brought needed goods to the Colonies and sent their own production overseas. America imported goods for consumption, and provided raw materials for manufacture. It exported goods to provide income for the producers. The American Colonies became regionalized in every respect, based on environmental factors. Farmers in each region had to learn what would grow and what they could export. In New England, little could grow, so its people had to create a non-agrarian economic system.

Most Colonial labor was farm labor, with only seven percent of the 1770 population located in cities of more than 2,500 inhabitants. Most family farms utilized family members for labor. Families were large, and each worked as a unit to achieve a standard of living. Few farms were commercial enterprises because too many factors hampered profitability. Those included supply shortages, poor production techniques, and scarcity of labor, even in large families. Transportation was also an obstacle, often preventing goods from reaching their markets efficiently.

Colonial farmers have often been criticized for being wasteful and unwilling to take steps to improve productivity, but their methods and practices were driven by an environment where land was cheaper than labor. Thomas Jefferson once commented, "You could buy a new acre for less money than it took to manure an old acre."[3] Over time, agriculture in the Colonies advanced through increased population, better investments, and differentiation of skills.

The value of exports from the Upper South amounted to £1 million pounds sterling for 1768-72, three-quarters of which were shipments of tobacco to Britain. The Lower South exported 550,000 pounds during the same period, of which sixty percent was rice and twenty percent was indigo. The Middle Colonies exported 520,000 pounds, of which sixty five percent were grain products. In New England during the same period, producers shipped 430,000 pounds, including thirty-five percent fish, twenty percent livestock, and fifteen percent wood products.

Colonists were consumers as well as producers, and consumption grew with the population, as Britain became more efficient at providing goods needed by the Americans. In 1700, yearly imports from Britain averaged £1 per capita or about 180,000 pounds in all. By 1770, imports were £1.2 per capita or about 3,000,000 pounds total. Products imported in the largest quantities included glass and earthenware, food, flannel, and wrought iron. Eighty percent of the goods imported were materials used in farming, reflecting the agricultural focus of the Colonial economy.

In general, the social classes in 18th Century America were duplicates of those in England, less the titles and certified lineage. An upper class in the Colonies, which emerged in the 17th Century, became mature in the 18th. Its members had acquired substantial wealth and lived lives of ease, although they were a small demographic and disorganized as a class. Geography helped define an upper-class Gentleman. In the South, he was a plantation owner living on an estate of several thousand acres. He grew rice or indigo and later, cotton. His primary work force consisted of slaves, and he employed an overseer to manage the property. With plenty of leisure time, the owner had to find activities to occupy the hours, such as sports, land speculation, political affairs, or military pursuits. He and his peers often dispensed justice as local magistrates and tried to influence the Colonial government, especially when it came to laws they regarded as counter to their interests.

In the Middle Colonies, large estates were a hallmark of the upper class. The proprietors were often the second generations of Dutch, Scottish, and English families that arrived in the Colonies in the middle of the 17th Century. Their estates were enormous, with as many as 200,000 acres in one property. Many of those men had taken over land formerly owned by the Dutch West India Company.

The upper class of New England emerged because their land would not support agriculture. The rich made money from merchandising and also from the return on their investments. They accumulated assets by building businesses, amassing profits and then putting money back into the businesses, or using it for investments. Profits were seldom less than fifty percent, so assets accrued quickly. A wealthy New Englander was often in the loan business, because there were no banks. He lent money over the short term and charged interest compounded semi-annually. He also financed real estate, provided he owned enough collateral.

Over time, as America grew, its cultural character began to emerge. There was a shared belief in equal opportunity for all and the need to work together to overcome the challenges of the wilderness. With abundant natural resources available, any man could succeed if he worked hard enough. This "American Character" opposed subservience to a king and parliament located three thousand miles away, especially when the interests of the British ran counter to their own.

Growing Independence

During the first half of the 18th Century, three factors set the stage for the march to independence. The first was the growing confidence of the American people, based on a robust economy, self-sufficiency, and the development of a unique national character. The second was the indifference of Britain toward the Colonies during the time when it had to face its own internal problems. Wars with France and Spain were serious; it was 1763 before Britain could bring her attention back to the Colonies in America. The third factor was the economic oppression driven by the English appetite for profit. As the English business interests tightened the screws, the Americans became angrier, more independent, and increasingly resistant to exploitation.

Soon after the conclusion of the French and Indian War, Americans started thinking seriously about independence. The French no longer posed a threat to western expansion, so the frontier did not require British protection. The crown saw no savings from withdrawing from the frontier, so it began to look for new sources of income. With vast, unexplored territory opened for settlement, new development required more money. The logical source for that money was taxing the Americans, because they were the beneficiaries of the settlements.

British Oppression

George Grenville, Minister for Management of the American Colonies, took the lead in looking for new revenue to help offset the enormous British debt. Grenville dispatched customs agents to the Colonies when he heard taxes were often uncollected. After putting an army of tax collectors in place, he resurrected the Molasses Act of 1733. Originally designed to stop the Colonies from trading with the French sugar islands, the act had never been enforced. Grenville knew enforcement would be ruinous to a major Colonial enterprise (rum), so he cut the tax in half and passed it in 1764 as the Sugar Act. Taking his plan a step further, Grenville passed the Stamp Act to become effective November 1, 1765. It required that the Colonies purchase stamps and affix them to all sorts of printed matter, including newspapers, pamphlets, college diplomas and insurance policies. Finally, Grenville passed the Quartering Act, which required the Colonies to supply provisions and shelter for British troops stationed in America.

Throughout 1765, there was a storm of protest across the Colonies. The Stamp Act was the main target because it represented taxation without representation, and offended all segments of Colonial American society, from lawyers, to printer-editors, to merchants and planters. Colonial newspapers attacked the Stamp Act through the winter of 1765-66 and Americans regarded the British as a move to take away their hard-earned liberty. They suspected the

British would soon use tax levies to support all Colonial governments and remove Colonial authority.

Although resistance to the Stamp Act was universal, the lower classes sought stronger measures of retaliation; they had no relationship with the crown, so their militant opposition helped create the grass roots momentum that would fuel a more active resistance to the British government.

In the North, many refused to use the stamps, and the colonial authorities closed the courts to prevent their use on legal documents. Southerners, for their part, completely ignored their existence. Boycotts of British goods began and grew stronger and the Colonists were encouraged to buy American-made goods. During this period, the Colonies cancelled orders for 600,000 pounds of British goods as a show of solidarity. Demonstrations occurred in Boston, organized by bands of men who called themselves "Sons of Liberty." Angry Colonists hounded stamp agents out of office and torched their facilities. Nine Colonies sent representatives to a Stamp Act Congress in October 1765 and prepared an important document with a very long title, *Rights and Grievances of the Colonies, A Petition to the King for Relief, and a Petition to Parliament for Repeal of the Stamp Act*. In March 1766, the British Parliament gave in, but then retaliated by passing the Declaratory Act, asserting Parliament's right to make laws that were binding on the Colonies. In the excitement of the Stamp Act repeal, the passage of the Declaratory Act went largely unnoticed.

For the next four years, British Parliament and its agents battled the Colonies; Parliament created additional acts to repress them and the Colonial citizens protested their enactment. The result was increasing unity in the Colonies, as people realized they had much more in common with each other than with their British masters. Events began to accelerate on March 5, 1770, after the Boston Massacre took place.

There had always been resentment in Boston against British troops quartered there, and on the day of the Massacre, a group of Colonists mocked and ridiculed a group of British soldiers. Someone fired a shot, and before the smoke cleared, five Colonists were dead and eight were injured. To cool things down, the British commander moved his troops out of Boston, but Colonists who had never spoken of independence before the massacre were now onboard with those already behind it. Three years later, in 1773, Lord North, the director of finance, conspired to bail out the East India Tea Company by sending tea to the Colonies and subsidizing it to make it cheaper for the Colonists to buy tea than for Englishmen. The plan was to allow the Tea Company to sell to retailers directly and bypass wholesalers they had used in the past, further increasing profits. To the Colonists, those efforts looked like a plot to monopolize trade and they protested. On December 16, 1773, a group of patriots in Boston boarded a merchant ship loaded with tea and dumped the cargo overboard. Some Colonists found the wanton destruction of property appalling, but then the British overplayed their hand.

Start of the Rebellion

In April 1774, Parliament passed four new laws designed to discipline the city of Boston. The most blatant of those so-called Coercive Acts, was the naming of a military governor for Massachusetts. Colonial reaction was swift and the first Continental Congress was called to meet September 5, 1774. Fifty-five delegates attended, representing all thirteen Colonies. The delegates found themselves divided into two factions: moderates, including

John Dickinson of Pennsylvania and John Jay of New York; and radicals, including Sam Adams and John Adams of Massachusetts and Patrick Henry of Virginia. The moderate group wanted to retain the benefits of the British Empire and protection from the democratic movement in the Colonies. Mostly lawyers, they disputed the rights of the Crown to impose some of its acts on the Colonies and claimed the Colonies were entitled to some autonomy. The radicals' dislike of British law was more important to them than their rights as citizens or their interest in the democratic movement. They were unorganized but driven by popular pressure, which strengthened their resolve to oppose the Crown.

The output of the Convention was a declaration of American rights, denying the right of Parliament to control internal affairs of the Colonies; there also was a petition for relief to the King. On October 20, 1774, the convention set up a Continental Association to begin an organized boycott of British goods. In November that year, Parliament declared Massachusetts in rebellion and forbade the Colonies of New England to trade with any nation outside the Empire.

The rest of the story is familiar to most Americans: the battles of Lexington and Concord took place in April 1775 and launched the Revolution. The Second Continental Congress of 1775 created a Federal government, and the Declaration of Independence was published in July of 1776. The Revolution lasted until the British surrendered in 1781. Two years later, a peace treaty officially recognized the Colonies as an independent nation, the United States of America.

The New Nation

The United States began as a new nation in 1776 and was a nation of independent-minded people, fueled by opportunity and liberty, seeking a government that would protect their right to the freedom they had secured. The moral basis of that right was liberty and freedom from oppression. America would soon build a political system based on protection from government overreach, with explicit focus on fairness, loyalty, and liberty.

Americans did not need protection from the wilderness; they could challenge it themselves and succeed or fail. They needed protection from evil government, whether it is their former British masters or a government they created for themselves. In their view, too much government was the enemy of freedom, so all governments had to have limits. The ultimate question for the Constitutional Convention to resolve was how to balance the role of government against any tendency toward anarchy.

CHAPTER SEVEN

ESTABLISHING AN AMERICAN GOVERNMENT

*The American Constitution was not written to protect
criminals; it was written to protect the government from
becoming criminals.*

Lenny Bruce

Soon after the Revolutionary War began in April 1775, the
Colonial leaders decided to convene a second Continental
Congress. Their goal was to create the basis for a
revolutionary government, because there was no existing
body for that purpose. The official document of that
Congress listed grievances against the Crown and the
necessity of taking up arms against it. One year later, the
Declaration of Independence was adopted on July 4, 1776.
Shortly after, a group of delegates started work on the
Articles of Confederation. The Articles created a legitimate
governmental structure for the new United States, but
debates and the war delayed their adoption until November
15, 1777.

The New Government

The new government created a confederation of states,
which recognized the sovereignty of its members, and

called for a League of Friendship between and among them for their protection and mutual welfare. The states could appoint between two and seven delegates to meet in Congress on the first Monday in November of each year to discuss any business of interest. Each state would have one vote on questions before the body. The states could not take certain actions without consent of the others, including forming treaties with foreign powers, setting up agreements between themselves, and declaring or becoming involved in war.

As soon as the new government was in operation, member states began to exploit its weaknesses. One of its major shortcomings was the absence of an executive, who would exert authority over the members. The states also struggled with the legalities of transferring property from the Colonial owners and the Crown to the United States. Perhaps the worst problem was the expropriation of private property (investments) through inflation. The Continental Congress had financed the war through issuing unsecured bills of credit and after it ended, they knowingly allowed inflation to render the bills worthless. The result was a total loss to the investors. Those and other problems caused Americans to question whether their new government could function effectively. It became obvious that fear of central authority was no worse than an uncontrolled democracy. The government needed to be restructured.

The Annapolis Conference was scheduled for September 1786 and was designed to bring together representatives from the states to discuss changes to the Articles of Confederation. James Madison was the prime mover for the conference and the Colony of Virginia sent out the call to order. Unfortunately, only five states sent delegations so, without a quorum, the attending delegates could not conduct any official business. They did use the occasion to discuss problems with the Articles and agreed to put together a larger convention the next summer in Philadelphia.

The Constitutional Convention

The Constitutional Convention began in Philadelphia on May 14, 1787. Fifty-five men attended, and thirty-nine signed the final draft of the Constitution, after the states voted to accept it. Thirty-five of the delegates were lawyers; twenty-nine had served in the Continental Army; eight were governors; and thirteen were merchants. Four of the delegates are familiar historical figures: George Washington, Benjamin Franklin, Alexander Hamilton and James Madison. Many assume that Thomas Jefferson was one of the framers, but he was serving as a Minister to France and missed the event. John Adams was also absent, serving as Ambassador to Great Britain.

The delegates elected George Washington president of the convention during the opening session and, although not an active participant, he created an air of stability that carried through the proceedings. Benjamin Franklin was eighty-one years old that summer but played a very active role. He never addressed the delegation, but made his opinions known by writing speeches and having them read aloud by others. His appeal for ratification at the end of the Convention was crucial to achieving a consensus among the delegates.

Hamilton was one of the staunchest supporters of the Federalist ideal, which asserted that a central government was crucial to overcome the excessive democracy of the states. Madison was equally important because of his moderate views. Sometimes referred to as "the Father of the Constitution," he did a great deal of research prior to the Convention and kept meticulous notes of the proceedings. After the Constitution was completed, Madison participated with Hamilton and John Jay in writing a collection of essays called the *Federalist Papers*. Those essays were successful in making the case for acceptance of the new government. Madison submitted seventeen amendments to the Constitution, including the ten that make up the Bill of Rights.

Several factions existed among the framers, based on their philosophical inclinations. The largest group, represented by Washington, Hamilton and Franklin, were the Nationalists. They believed government must force people to cooperate for the public good, or else they would put themselves ahead of the interests of all. Washington contributed a plan for training a class of professional politicians to govern by representing the highest ideals of government. The opposing group was the Republican ideologues, who retained the belief that a government could be founded on classical Republican principles which focused on public virtue. James Madison was not committed to any single ideology, but remained open to any design that would overcome the problems of the Articles. A study of the comments he made during the Convention, and afterward in the *Federalist Papers*, reveals Madison was initially a supporter of a purely national government with no state participation whatsoever. He thought laws passed by the national government should act on individuals directly, rather than through the states. As a practical man, Madison modified his views during the Constitutional process, once he understood how the new government needed to be structured.

Delegates at the Convention knew what was at stake: the future of the Republic and the prevention of anarchy. Most agreed that the Articles of Confederation were too weak to be effective and needed revision. How to revise them was the question. The characters of the delegates, who varied widely in experience, points of view, and willingness to participate, complicated the process of designing a new government. Some delegates never spoke a word during the entire Convention, while Governor Morris of Pennsylvania gave 173 speeches. Remarkably, no faction dominated the proceedings because moderate points of view offset extreme positions and the moderates regularly shifted from one side to the other.

The delegates were educated men who were experienced in politics. Many were well versed in ancient history, as well as the history of governments, and all were familiar with the British system. They had read the major philosophers on government, including Hume and Locke. In the end, the delegates had to go where no government had gone before. They had to find a balance between the smaller political units of the states and a centralized federal system. They knew that ancient Rome had no states and had encountered great difficulty exerting control over a large territory, so they had to find a way to avoid that problem.

Advancing the Concept of a Republic

The framers gave a lot of attention to the concept of Republics and their application in the United States. Because of the excesses of King George III, they were not interested in any form of government that included a monarch. Opinions varied regarding the structure of a republic, ranging from a free government that relied on the morality and integrity of the populace to one where property served as the guarantor of virtue.

Those from New England tended to favor the former position because of its compatibility with the Puritan philosophy. They embraced the concept of public virtue based on firmness, courage, industry, frugal living, and devotion to the goals of government.

Those from outside New England took the opposite position. They believed personal virtue was dangerous because it relied too much on the individual. It was better to build public virtue and use it to control the weakness of individuals. They believed ownership of land and the freedom it created for people created public virtue. An individual could live his life independently, so long as he was vigilant and aware of threats to the Republic.

From a structural standpoint, the framers wanted a balanced political system that protected liberty through the participation of the people. An executive branch would balance the disorganization of the legislature, but the legislature would act on behalf of the people against the executive. The experience of creating the Articles of Confederation had convinced them of the need for a strong executive who could get things done in a timely fashion. To overcome their fear of tyranny, they would create a system of checks and balances to limit the power of the executive.

The great debates of the Convention dealt with the design of the Legislative Branch, the Presidency, and the purpose and authority of the Convention itself. Arguments over the structure of the legislature consumed the most time and posed the greatest threat to the success of the proceeding. Small states felt the need to protect their interests in a national government and were willing to quit the Convention if those protections were not included. Small states, in that instance, were states without claims to western land, including Connecticut, New Jersey, New York, Delaware, Rhode Island, New Hampshire, and Maryland. The large states were Massachusetts,

Pennsylvania, Virginia, North Carolina, South Carolina and Georgia.

The initial plan for government, introduced by Edmund Randolph of Virginia, called for the creation of a federal government consisting of a legislative branch made up of two bodies with members chosen from the states by popular vote; an executive branch; and a separate judicial branch, all setup along the structural lines outlined by the French political philosopher Montesquieu. As the delegates heard the plan, it became obvious to them that it went much further than a simple modification of the Articles.

As the debate got underway, the method of electing Congressmen was the first item on the agenda. The Randolph Plan called for the election of members of the house by popular vote, which immediately set off arguments. The Delaware delegation warned they would walk out of the Convention if the one vote per state used in the Articles were discarded. Many opposed popular vote, favoring selection by state legislatures. Eldridge Gerry of Massachusetts stated:

"The evils we experience flow from an excess of democracy. The people do not want virtue, but are the dupes of pretended patriots. In Massachusetts, it has been fully confirmed by experience that they are daily misled by false reports circulated by designing men, and which no one on the spot can refute."[4] On the opposing side was George Mason of Virginia who, according to Madison's notes:

"Argued strongly for the election of the larger branch by the people. It was the grand depository of the democratic principles of government to let the people vote." [5] Madison himself felt that the election of representatives by the legislatures moved the people too far from their government.

After tabling the debate on voting for house members on May 31, 1787 and reaching no consensus again on June 6th, the delegates decided to take up debate over the method of the election of senators. The proposal was their election by popular vote. This recommendation brought an angry reaction from the small states and it came to a head June 9, when David Brearly of New Jersey explained the position of the small states regarding the legislature. He pointed out that if the apportionment plan was adopted, it would produce three large states and ten small ones. Virginia would have sixteen legislators and Georgia would have one, creating a situation in which the large states could always force their positions on the small states. The delegates took a day off on June 10, and when they reconvened the following day, Roger Sherman of Connecticut offered a compromise.

As it is now known, the Connecticut (or Great) Compromise called for a modification in the way members of the two houses of the legislature were elected; the house seats would be apportioned based on population and the senate posts would have an equal vote for one senator per state. The convention rejected the Connecticut plan that day, but the debate continued, and a compromise plan was adopted on July 16. Since the delegates were already familiar with the legislatures in their own states, they were aware of the need for checks and balances among the branches. That realization made debates on legislative structure less raucous than debates on ideology had been. The structure for separation of powers, along with checks and balances, satisfied each faction's delegates for specific reasons. The aristocrats, like Hamilton, distrusted the people, and felt that non-property owners would become pawns of the rich and would vote as they were told. The republicans took the opposite view and believed the checks would prevent too much centralization in government, and prevent a push toward monarchy.

The same ideological differences were evident in the debates over the presidency. Most delegates believed an executive was necessary and must be separate from the legislative and judicial branches, but they disagreed about the span of authority. A dozen delegates feared executive power for what it could become and advocated a system with multiple executives. Those who took an opposite point of view feared that one executive would not be strong enough to offset the power of the legislature. On June 1, 1787 when the debate on the executive began, Edmund Randolph vigorously opposed the concept of a single executive, calling it "the fetus of monarchy." [6] James Wilson of Pennsylvania stated that the single executive was the best safeguard against tyranny. James Madison asked the convention to move on to the method of choosing the executive, hoping that controls placed there that would assuage the fears of the Republicans. The initial decision called for the executive to be elected by the legislature and serve one seven-year term. The delegates agreed on that concept, allowing the discussion to return to the number of executives. The delegates agreed to one executive on June 4, 1787.

The structure of the judicial branch was not a contentious issue. Most of the framers agreed on the general principles of its structure and saw it as the least powerful branch. They voted to create the judiciary as an independent entity, with lifelong appointments for judges, premised on good behavior. Judges would face impeachment and removal from office if they committed egregious acts or crimes. Equally important was the fundamental principle of allowing the courts to strike down legislative acts that violated the Constitution. Some delegates even supported having the court veto legislation, based on policy grounds in addition to Constitutional grounds, but the delegates rejected that power. The Convention created the judicial review provision by adopting the following nebulous wording,

"This Constitution, and the Laws of the United States which shall be made in Pursuance thereof; and all Treaties made, or which shall be made, under the Authority of the United States, shall be the supreme Law of the Land; and the Judges in every State shall be bound thereby, any thing in the Constitution or Laws of any State to the Contrary notwithstanding."[7]

The judiciary section left out the creation of lower federal courts because of arguments about interfering with state courts; later, the creation of those courts was included under the powers and control of Congress. The Convention also added the right for Congress to approve Supreme Court justices.

With the most contentious issues resolved, the Convention proceeded smoothly. A subcommittee on details worked on the document from August 27, 1787 until completed on September 14 of that year. Then, on September 17, the Secretary of the Convention read the Constitution to the delegates. All states except South Carolina approved. There were no delegates, and no votes from Rhode Island. Of the framers who did not vote, six left the Convention early for diverse reasons, and two were not present at the signing. After attempts to warn those unwilling to sign about the danger of their refusals, the supporters gave up. All signed the signatory document except Edmund Randolph and George Mason of Virginia and Elbridge Gerry of Massachusetts. Gerry feared civil war and said his state was full of contentious factions, for and against the constitutional process. Gerry wished that the Constitution were in a more "mediating shape" with respect to the Articles.

Despite the disagreements and arguments, the framers produced a unique historical document, born out of the influence of history and the recent experiences with their own political system. From a single-branched, weak confederation, they produced a four-branched (including the states), interconnected political system that compromised separation of powers for the sake of checks and balances. Every previous national government had been either centralized or had been a confederation of sovereign states. The man who created the final design, John Dickinson, justified the part national, part federal system with the following words, "The territory of such extent as the United America could not be safely and advantageously governed, but by a combination of republics, each retaining all the rights of supreme sovereignty excepting such as ought to be contributed to the union." [8]

Sovereignty

Of course, the architecture of the new government created a new theoretical problem concerning sovereignty, the question being how the states could be sovereign inside the sovereign United States. Hamilton answered that question in *Federalist 34* when he spoke of the unique types of Roman assemblies. He described the differences between the role and function of the Roman Republic's Comitia Centuriata and the Comitia Tributa, which were not branches of the same legislature but were different legislatures.

One critical issue not addressed at the Convention, was the Bill of Rights. On September 11, 1787, Gerry made a motion to have the committee on detail prepare a Bill of Rights but the motion was defeated unanimously. One gets the sense, reading Madison's notes, that the delegates lacked the energy to accomplish that goal. As the Convention neared the end of its four-month session, its participants suffered from the overwhelming effects of the Philadelphia summer, each day confined together in a single room with the windows closed so no one could overhear the debate.

The Constitution paved the way for the American democracy to proceed. But was it really a democracy? Certainly not in the Greek sense of the term. The United States was to be a "federation of Republics," the Republics being the states. It was also a representational democracy, requiring that the people elect representatives to protect their interests. The effort to produce a new government was driven by the urgency of the times and distrust of the English Crown. The founders had faced the challenge of discovering the right model that would prevent both anarchy and tyranny. In the end, they created a unique model that would become a standard for the Western World.

The Delicate Balance of Power

As stated, the United States Constitution was a product of its time, filtered through the American Colonial experience. Once the Revolution was won, the founders began to create the new government but "power" as a key theoretical concept generated sharp disagreements when incorporated into a new form of government. Madison's notes, from the Constitutional convention, give a sense of the ideological divide over the seat of power in the new government. Should power reside with the people or the central government? The first was frightful because it could lead to rule of a mob. The second was equally scary because accumulated power could lead to tyranny. With these concerns in mind, the framers devised to a model with an excess of controls, which would prevent the misuse of power but could also deadlock the American government and keep it from addressing the problems it would need to solve.

The Progressives' Perspective

Are the Progressives right in tarring the founders as elitists who cared nothing for the common people? They are not. Colonial America was a society of individuals and families, not special interest groups. The framers created the Constitution to protect individuals from government, which was the tradition of the Enlightenment. The Revolution had created a united American psyche that merged into pursuit of the American dream, free from the oppression of government.

The Constitutional convention was held only two years before the French Revolution. America's leaders were seeking an Enlightenment world that supported individual rights against government. Corporations and corporate exploitation were off in the future. Socialism was barely an idea. The framers replaced the Articles of Confederation with a more complete model of government because they knew the Articles were not working. Washington's hope that the Constitution would last twenty-five years tells us he knew the document was imperfect and expected it to evolve.

Progressive activity in early America was relegated to working on a small scale, at the local level, to help those in need. This was a logical extension of Christian beliefs and the colonist's experience back in Europe. In time, Colonial legislatures and state governments adopted legislation patterned after English laws. These laws would establish an American tradition of public responsibility for the care of the poor.

CHAPTER EIGHT

GAINING LEGITIMACY

We are now forming a republican government. Real liberty is never found in despotism or the extremes of democracy, but in moderate governments.

Alexander Hamilton

The period following the Constitutional Convention was one of the most critical in American history. A group of idealistic men had just welded together our Colonial experience, the British Constitution, lessons of antiquity, and contemporary political theory to produce a new model of government. It was a not just a new government for a new nation; it was the first new nation in perhaps fifteen hundred years. Would it succeed? The answer to that question depended on the ability of the new government to earn the trust of the American people.

Max Weber (1864-1920), the great German sociologist, wrote about power, authority, and bureaucracy in political systems. Weber described three ways for a government to gain legitimacy: tradition, charismatic leadership, and rational-legal authority. Tradition, the oldest of the forms and the most familiar to us, describes hereditary monarchies and their leader's "right to rule," inherited from his predecessors. Tradition engendered comfort through the appearance of stability, but like all types of political power, it had to be effective to survive. The British monarchs saw their power steadily erode over the centuries because of corrupt practices and incompetence. Each time a monarch proved unworthy, parliament transferred power to themselves, until the monarchy reached a point where it was powerless.

Charismatic leadership, according to Weber, was the opposite of traditional leadership. It was short term and based on one person's ability to influence others through strength of personality. Its great limitation was mortality, because there was no replacement when the leader was gone. Charismatic leaders had the strongest impact on societies because they united people through an emotional response that supported actions the leader took.

Weber's third type, rational-legal authority, described a system that selected political leaders through a legally sanctioned procedure. The modern American government is a prime example of that type, because it validates legitimacy every two years at election time. If voters are satisfied that elections are fair, they grant the power to rule.

Because the United States had no previous hereditary government and no elections to demonstrate the people's approval, it had to rely on charismatic leaders to produce legitimacy. Those who aspired to lead the country were the same men that designed the government, so they lacked provable credibility. Moreover, the government was too isolated from the people to gain a consensus of public opinion and the public had not participated in the Constitutional process. It took the charisma of Washington and sustained efforts by Jefferson, Hamilton, and Madison to unite the people behind the new government. Unlike the Roman Republic, Americans knew their rights and were willing to use force, if necessary, to maintain them. That put pressure on the framers, who realized the value

Washington as the charismatic leader required to gain credibility for the new political system. The new government was on trial, so Washington had to be visible as the leader of the nation.

Weber argued that charismatic leaders had exceptional value because they helped mask disruptive elements that appeared when an institution was in transition. That was certainly true in Washington's case. With no guide for how to govern the new country, he had to figure out a way to move smoothly into the new system, so the people could see that their government was effective.

The effort to gain legitimacy began the day after the convention ended on September 17, 1787. The new Constitution required ratification by a majority of the states before it could be implemented, so Congress sent copies to the States in late September. Around the same time, an article critical of the Constitution appeared in the New York press. Its author used the pseudonym Cato. A second critical article appeared under the name Brutus on October 18. Alexander Hamilton, sensing a risk to ratification, composed the first of the *Federalist Papers*, to defend the Constitution. Hamilton used the pseudonym Publius and his article appeared in three New York newspapers on October 27, 1787. *Federalist One* vigorously defended the Constitution against the Articles of Confederation and predicted that complaints would continue, even though the criticisms were unfounded.

For the remainder of the fall of 1787, Federalists and anti-Federalists were publishing essays, putting important arguments in front of the American people. Critics who believed the Constitution did not offer enough protections for the people made compelling arguments for a bill of rights. Three states, New York, Massachusetts, and Virginia said they would not vote for ratification until a bill of rights was put into place. Hamilton and Madison were opposed to a bill of rights, believing it unnecessary, but they could see that ratification was in jeopardy without it. Madison switched positions and promised the States that he would create and support a bill of rights.

In December 1787, the first three states, Delaware, Pennsylvania, and New Jersey voted to ratify. Georgia and Connecticut followed in January 1788. That left the Constitution three votes short of acceptance. Hamilton and Madison continued to print new Federalist essays throughout 1788, making the case for ratification. Massachusetts voted yes in February 1788, based on the promise that a Bill of Rights was forthcoming. Maryland and South Carolina ratified in April and May. Those states had secured the majority, but Hamilton and Madison continued to work on the big states of Virginia and New York, because of their influence. The Constitution was finally adopted on July 2, 1788, after Virginia ratified in June.

In June of the next year, Madison submitted a Bill of Rights, consisting of seventeen amendments, selected from one hundred suggested by the States. In August, the House approved the seventeen amendments and sent them to the Senate, where the list was cut to twelve. On September 24, 1789, Congress sent twelve amendments to the States for ratification. The States rejected two, but approved the others by December 15, 1791, making the Bill of Rights an official part of the Constitution.

National Leadership

The imposing figure of George Washington anchored the center of the Republic and was everyone's choice as the first President. The national leadership wanted to establish credibility as quickly as possible. Immediately following the ratification of the Constitution by New Hampshire in June 1788, the process of electing a President was set in motion. Congress passed an election ordinance on September 13th, which set January 7, 1789, as elector selection day and February 4th, as the day of the Presidential and Vice-Presidential vote. North Carolina and Rhode Island had not ratified the Constitution by that date, so they did not select any electors and did not participate. New York did not pass an election act in time to send electors.

When the votes were counted on February 4th, Washington received sixty-nine electoral votes, and was elected President. John Adams received thirty-four votes, making him Vice President. Washington lobbied for Adams because their political views were similar and Adams balanced the ticket geographically as a native of Massachusetts. Only thirty-four votes were from states where the people chose electors. America had elected its first president with less than half of the votes coming from representatives of the people.

Washington was very careful in developing his relations with Congress; he wanted to make sure to exercise the strength of his office without trying to dictate policy to the legislature. He sent messages with suggestions to Congress but did not offer an opinion on what course to take. He would not permit Congressional committees to solicit his opinion but he was willing to express his views "when asked." The first Congress went through its entire session without a single suggestion from the President. Eventually, an indirect channel was created between the Congress and Alexander Hamilton, who had no reservations whatsoever about making his opinions known. Hamilton became the de facto floor leader of the House and spent considerable time there in consultation with the members and attending committee hearings. After Hamilton resigned, the communications between the Executive branch and Congress were less frequent.

Although some had urged Washington to become an autocratic leader, he was too dedicated to the principles of the Republic to consider that option. He saw himself as a transition leader and hoped to retire in 1792, but the growing rift between Hamilton and Jefferson was too serious to ignore, so he had to stay on to maintain stability. The conflict between Hamilton and Jefferson would eventually lead to factionalism within the national government and the formation of political parties.

Hamilton perceived, early on, that one of the keys to government success was forging alliances with men of wealth. In his mind, democracy was unworkable because it would always lead to anarchy. He despised public opinion and told Washington that he considered it "of no value." By the time the Revolution ended, Hamilton had arrived at his own model of government, which included strength supported by wealth, and sustained, if need be, by a standing army.

Jefferson had missed the Constitutional Convention and did not take part in the debate over the new government. Given his Republican views, the Constitutional process might have been more difficult and the resulting government different.

Madison, then a Congressman from Virginia, aspired to the Senate, but Patrick Henry, the state's governor, blocked his nomination. Madison had been a key ally of Hamilton during the Constitutional Convention and worked together with him on the *Federalist Papers*. Madison retained strong points of view on the logic behind the separation of the powers of the Federal government, which would eventually cause him to break with Hamilton, whom Madison thought was redefining the powers in a dangerous way.

Jefferson, Madison, Hamilton and Political Parties

Between the spring of 1791 and all of 1792, Jefferson and Madison attacked Hamilton's authority, successfully blocking his ability to move forward. Hamilton's intrigues against Jefferson were equal in vigor. In late 1791, President Washington attempted to reconcile the two men, but could find no common ground. Jefferson resigned on July 31, 1793, after failing to garner support for France in their war with the English. Hamilton served until January 31, 1795.

When the wars between France and England broke out, the American factions took sides: The Democratic-Republicans of Jefferson for the French; and the Federalists of Hamilton for the British. The Federalists were convinced that the Democratic-Republicans were employing French agents to help overthrow the American government, and the Democratic-Republicans were convinced that the Federalists were conspiring with the English government to take over the United States.

After Washington signed the Jay Treaty in 1794, the Democratic-Republicans used popular indignation to rally against the policies of the Federalists, but both parties were still weak and could not overcome regional differences and take control. These regional differences drove several attempts by states to secede from the Union. Both Northern and Southern states threatened secession in the first decade of the United States' history. After losing office in 1801, some Federalist leaders even tried to take New England out of the Union in 1804 and 1808.

With the end of George Washington's second term approaching, the country was about to lose its charismatic leader and would have to rely on legitimacy through the popular vote of the people. Political division was a continuing threat to stability, as the Federalists and Democratic-Republicans continued to attack each other.

As the election of 1796 drew near, Hamilton sought to pull the strings of the Federalists and influence the election. John Adams was the Federalist choice for the next president because Hamilton was not ready. He needed time to recover his image from the damage done during his tenure as Secretary of the Treasury. Hamilton was still carrying a grudge toward Adams for having his father-in-law removed as Commander of the Saratoga campaign during the Revolution, so he hoped to prevent Adams' election. Thomas Pinckney of South Carolina was an obvious choice for vice-President, but Hamilton urged Southern electors to vote for Pinckney for President and a lessor candidate for Vice President, ignoring Adams all together. Adams' supporters from New England uncovered the plot and withheld their support of Pinckney as Vice President, causing him to drop to third place in the voting behind Adams and Jefferson.

This left the country with a President and Vice President from different parties. Jefferson himself almost threw away the election by attempting to use French support of his candidacy as a campaign issue. The electors did not take kindly to a foreign power trying to influence an American election.

Transition in Power

When the second Presidential election was over and the battle lines were drawn between the factions, it remained for the Democratic-Republicans to define their role as the opposition in American politics. During Washington's first term, bickering was under control because the main protagonists, Hamilton and Jefferson, were both serving in the cabinet. After Jefferson's withdrawal in 1793, the opposition became more open. Hamilton saw the Federalists as the government party, qualified to govern at the national level as opposed to the state level. Because they were anti-National, it made sense for the Democratic-Republicans to go directly to the people for support and take positions opposite to the national government. Those positions caused the Federalists to label Democratic-Republicans the champions of the uninformed masses and seditious.

Things reached a head in 1798 with the passage of the Alien and Sedition Acts, which represented an attempt to control criticism of the government. The law defined high misdemeanors as "to combine and conspire in order to oppose the legal measures of the government... or to publish a false or malicious writing against the government of the United States."[9] Democratic-Republicans were the targets, and all those arrested for violating the law were members of that party. Jefferson and Madison attempted to counter the Sedition Act by passing nullification ordinances through state legislatures that granted states the right to limit national authority within their borders.

The Federalist efforts against democracy played a significant role in the election of the Democratic-Republicans in 1800. Throughout Adams' term of office, the Democratic-Republicans conducted a grass roots campaign to identify target constituencies and turn them, while the Federalists fought among themselves. Hamilton's dislike of Adams weakened the Federalists' cause, while Jefferson and his supporters were piling on Adams for his poor performance as President; they blamed him for nearly going to war with France, and for his support of the Jay Treaty and the Sedition Acts. The tide had begun to turn in Congress. The third Congress of 1793-94 included forty-five Federalists and thirty-eight Democratic-Republicans. After the election of the fourth Congress in 1795, there were fifty-five Democratic-Republicans and thirty-six Federalists.

The election of 1800 saw Jefferson and Burr, both Democratic-Republicans, tied in electoral votes so the House of Representatives had to determine the outcome of that election. The house voted thirty-six times and Jefferson was elected with the powerful influence of Hamilton, who disliked Burr. The Federalists were out, never to return. That election also marked the first transition of power in American history. The dissolution of the Federalist power paved the way for Democratic-Republican rule for almost thirty years, until the election of Andrew Jackson in 1829.

The First Republican Party

Remember that the Republican Party of Jefferson we refer to here was not the Republican Party of Lincoln. It was an agrarian party, which was opposed central government. When the Federalist Party disappeared about 1815, the United States entered a brief period of party harmony because the Democratic-Republicans had no opposition. They controlled the Presidency through the elections of James Madison, James Monroe, and John Quincy Adams. Then, during Quincy Adam's presidency, Martin Van Buren built a "new" Democratic Party, which dropped the word Republican from its name, and nominated Andrew Jackson to be its first presidential candidate. The new Democrats took some of the philosophy of Jefferson's party but also emphasized the sovereignty of the people and majority rule.

This period of stability, which lasted through the first three decades of the nineteenth century, was essential for getting the new country on its feet and establishing the Constitution. Madison and Monroe, who followed Jefferson, carried the credibility of being Founding Fathers with them to the Presidency, and that was an additional stabilizing influence. Ultimately, the Democratic-Republicans could not win the favor of the elites, nor gain their support in replacement of the Federalists, unless there was a payoff. In other words, the Republicans had to find a way to foster economic development of the country in ways that would benefit landowners and merchants.

Jefferson tried to build a national program of business development but his efforts foundered; the States were not willing to give up what they saw as their responsibility to regulate business on their own. The States wanted the freedom to build their own infrastructure (roads, etc.), set up lotteries for construction projects, enact inspection standards, and enforce protectionist standards to allow businesses to get on their feet without serious competition. Ultimately, the people granted the government legitimacy because it was working.

Three great forces had converged to create a strong merchant mentality: the philosophy of the American businessmen strengthened over the time of the Colonial period; the economic efforts of Alexander Hamilton; and the realization on the part of National politicians that it was important for them to support business as part of their role as leaders.

The Democratic-Republican Party grew out of an opposition role as the anti-National party, despite it's having no program other than to oppose the Federalists. By building a popular base, the Democratic-Republicans succeeded in taking control of the government, but they never really mastered the art of moving to the center, which required accepting the importance of capitalist institutions in America.

Historical Perspective

The Framers of the United States Constitution did not anticipate the formation of political parties, which came into existence soon after the new government was put into operation. They knew about, and feared political factions, as Madison pointed out in *Federalist 10,* as follows:

> Among the numerous advantages promised by a well-constructed Union, none deserves to be more accurately developed than its tendency to break and control the violence of faction... The inference to which we are brought is, that the CAUSES of faction cannot be removed, and that relief is only to be sought in the means of controlling its EFFECTS. If a faction consists of less than a majority, relief is supplied by the republican principle, which enables the majority to defeat its sinister views by regular vote... When a majority is included in a faction, the form of popular government, on the other hand, enables it to sacrifice to its ruling passion or interest both the public good and the rights of other citizens[10]

The development of political parties in the Unites States was inevitable but was accelerated by the conflict between Hamilton and Jefferson. Each man was passionate and committed to his own ideology: Hamilton to a strong central government, and Jefferson to a democracy controlled by the people. Today, political parties are a fact of life in America; for better or worse.

CHAPTER NINE

THE PROGRESSIVE MOVEMENT IN THE UNITED
STATES 1870-1920

*Capitalism is the astounding belief that the wickedest of
men will do the wickedest of things for the greatest good of
everyone.*

John Maynard Keynes

The word "Progressive," like many other political-
philosophical terms, has a confused usage based on its
several definitions. The political Right uses the word as a
pejorative, while the Left equates it with efforts to achieve
Nirvana or Utopia. Today, the word retains great
popularity, because it stands for action to achieve social
justice and serves as a substitute for the discredited Liberal
philosophy.

Progressives today are typically members of the
Democratic Party who sit on the ideological Left of
Liberals. They believe there is more to making progress
than passing laws that benefit their own constituencies;
they want to alter the American political system to remove
its fundamental defects. These defects flow from an evil
capitalist economic system, which has been unrestrained
because of a poorly designed Constitution. Like any idea
that becomes a movement, Progressives have navigated
waves of acceptance and rejection as the American political

landscape changed over time. In periods when their efforts were blocked, Progressives employed a strategy that kept their movement alive. Today they prosper as the key political philosophy of the Left.

Preliminaries in the United States and Europe

In the period, from 1800 to 1870, there was enormous economic expansion in the United States, as the country established itself as a global economic power. The country's total area of 360,000 square miles in 1800 was ten times that size by 1900. Economic growth drove the accumulation of wealth; there was tremendous exploitation of natural resources; industrialization grew unchecked; and transportation systems were created to operate the Capitalist engine. During that period, the American worker's level of productivity increased significantly, further driving expansion of the Capitalist economy. In addition, expansion led to misconduct as corporations took advantage of their unregulated freedom to exploit the American worker, farmer, or small businessman. Their conduct raised a cry of revolt that would create the first implementation of the Progressive ideology in the United States.

In Europe, the situation was quite different. Socialism, acting as an alternate model of Progressive ideology, originated at the time of the French Revolution and came into full bloom during the Industrial Age. Initially, its aim was to tear down feudalism and expand democracy, but later the poverty and inequality resulting from Capitalist exploitation drove socialists to see government action as the only way to end worker abuse.

Socialism began as a set of ideas around collectivism or joint ownership of property. Utopian thinkers such as Robert Owen (1771-1858) and Charles Fourier (1772-1837) created Utopian community models, but were unable to achieve any long-term success with them. They had hoped their models would demonstrate that a careful adoption of Utopian systems could gradually transform a society. Social democratic parties grew out of this early socialist thinking, but they preached a more activist approach than the utopians had taken. To the Socialists, activism meant transitioning governments to Socialist models featuring government control of production. Even more radical were the Anarchists like Bakunin and his followers who advocated the overthrow of all governments.

The flashpoint of this initial period of Progressivism was the Revolutions of 1848, which affected some fifty sovereign states in Europe. Those revolts were essentially democratic in nature and sought to remove the last vestiges of the feudal system to create independent national states. For European nationalists, 1848 was the springtime of hope, when they thought that newly emerging nationalities would reject the old multinational empires. They were bitterly disappointed when the revolts failed. Afterward, many governments engaged in a partial reversal of the revolutionary reforms, as well as heightening repression and censorship. In the decade after 1848, little had visibly changed in Europe, and many historians have considered the entire Revolution of 1848 a failure.

Nevertheless, there were some successes when Austria and Prussia eliminated feudalism by 1850 and Russia freed their serfs in 1861. The first major union in Germany, the Social Democratic Workers' Party, was founded in 1869 under the influence of Marx and Engels. In 1875, it merged with the General German Workers' Association to become what is known today as the German

Social Democratic Party (SPD). In Germany, Austria, and France, Socialist parties and Anarchists played a prominent role in forming and building trade unions, especially from the 1870s onward. German unions applied enough pressure on their government to force Bismarck to initiate the German welfare state in 1884.

Progressive Action Begins in the United States

Progressivism in the United States began as a populist movement in rural America. The economic trigger occurred after 1873, when farm prices fell under the weight of overproduction. Farmers felt burdened by exorbitant railroad shipping charges and excessive interest on the money they borrowed for working capital. By the early 1880s, Grange organizations, which were created initially as social clubs, became more militant. They grew into farmer alliances, which were a kind of union that coalesced and began electing political candidates who would work on their behalf in state legislatures. Those efforts failed, so the farmer alliances took their complaints to the Federal government. That tactic worked, despite corporate opposition. In 1887, Congress created the Interstate Commerce Commission and it regulated trade practices that crossed state lines, and limited the overcharges of the railroads.

The farmers' economic pain subsided with the boom of 1897, but the time was ripe for accelerating the pace of other efforts by the Progressive Movement, which had been at work for some time. The catalyst for that effort had two components: the exploitation of Americans by business; and the criminal activities of corrupt politicians.

Progressive action expanded when the common people formed a grassroots movement powerful enough to push back on the political system and to force legislatures to take action against abuses of money and power. The abuses were so egregious that the drive for much-needed changes arose like waves across the country; once in action, no robber baron or corrupt politician could withstand or stop the momentum. Key objectives were revised; child labor laws were enacted; and protections for women in the workplace were put in place, along with a minimum wage for working women.

During the last two decades of the 19th Century, workers in the States were influenced by events happening in Europe. Immigrants, who had been exposed to Socialist unions there, wanted to see the same organizations operating in their new country. The Socialist Labor Party of America (SPA) was founded in 1877. Later, in 1901, a new organization called the Socialist Party of America was created and became highly successful for a time under labor organizer and socialist leader Eugene Debs (1855-1926). The Socialist party in America grew to 150,000 members in 1912 and polled 900,000 in that year's Presidential campaign. At one time, the SPA boasted 33 city mayors, many seats in state legislatures, and two members of the United States House of Representatives.

The Socialist Party formed strong alliances with several labor unions because they shared similar goals. The most prominent U.S. unions at that time included the American Federation of Labor (AFL), the Knights of Labor (KoL), and the Industrial Workers of the World (IWW). In 1869, Uriah S. Stephens founded the Noble and Holy Order of the Knights of Labor, employing secrecy and fostering a semireligious aura to "create a sense of solidarity." The Knights comprised "one big union of all workers." In 1886, a convention of delegates from twenty separate unions formed the AFL, with Samuel Gompers as its head. The IWW followed a similar path after it formed in 1905.

The Socialist movement gained strength from its ties to labor. The panic of 1907, along with the growing strength of the Socialists and trade unions, sped up the process of reform. Corporations, acting against those efforts, sought to protect their profits by taking direct action against unions and strikers. They hired strikebreakers and pressured the government to call in the National Militia when workers refused to do their jobs. Numerous workers' strikes dissolved into violent confrontations.

Progressive Intellectuals

Those who stood against Capitalism in the United States were influenced by the writings of Progressive intellectuals who constructed a theoretical foundation for the movement during its initial period. Henry George (1839-1897), a political economist, looked at land speculation as a destroyer of wealth because it raised the price of land faster than the economic output of the land could increase. That meant less and less capital was available for wages and profit, pushing people toward bankruptcy. As an alternative, George proposed a single tax on land values that was a tax on the annual value of land held as private property. It would be made high enough to allow for all other taxes, especially those on labor and production, to be abolished. George argued that a land value tax would give owners an incentive to use land in a productive way, by putting people to work and creating wealth. This shift in the bargaining balance between resource owners and laborers would raise the general level of wages and ensure no one would suffer involuntary poverty. George also advocated for other Progressive-like programs, including the municipalization of utilities, free trade, the secret ballot, universal pension, bankruptcy protection, and women's suffrage.

It would be difficult to overstate Henry George's impact on reform movements operating at the turn of the 20th Century and Progressivism. George's book *Progress and Poverty* was widely popular, and its publication is often marked as the beginning of the Progressive Era. George's message attracted broad support across the political spectrum, including union activists, Socialists and Conservatives.

Lester Ward (1841-1913) published his two volume *Dynamic Sociology--Or Applied Social Science as Based upon Statistical Sociology and the Less Complex Sciences* in 1883. His aim was to re-introduce the scientific method to the field of sociology. Ward asserted that man should not consider himself helpless before the forces of nature and evolution; he should instead direct the evolution of human culture using science. Through sociology, there should emerge a universal and comprehensive system of education, regulation of competition, connection of people together based on equal opportunities and cooperation, and promotion of the happiness and the freedom of everyone.

Edward Bellamy (1850-1898) was famous for a single book that had a significant impact on Progressive thought. It was the Utopian science fiction novel, *Looking Backward, 2000–1887,* published in January 1888. The novel captured the imagination of the American reading public and made Bellamy a household name. The story revolved around Julian West, son of an aristocratic family, who was placed into a deep hypnotic sleep by a Dr. Pillsbury and survived in that state for one hundred years. He was awakened in the year 2000. Julian was shocked to see how society had changed in his absence. The economy was run by public rather than private capital, the government controlled the means of production, and profits were divided equally among all citizens. Each person received a college degree and all retired at age forty-five. At the end of the book, Julian experienced a nightmare that he was back in the year 1887, back to a society of inequality and corruption.

Bellamy's book sold 200,000 copies the first year of publication and by the end of the 19th Century had sold more copies than every other American book, except *Uncle Tom's Cabin*. Bellamy stated he did not write *Looking Backward* to stimulate political action; he intended it to be a "literary fantasy," his vision of a country relieved of its social problems. That vision could be realized through the elimination of competition and establishment of state ownership of industry. Both ideas were appealing to Progressives fighting the inequality of the Gilded Age. Bellamy became active in the Progressive Movement he helped create when he founded his own magazine, *The New Nation*, in 1891. For three years, he toured the country, speaking to members of Nationalist Clubs that were founded in response to *Looking Back*.

Corrupt City Governments

In the mid-1890s, the Progressive Movement maintained momentum through the rulings of judges and the writings of "muckraker" journalists. The term "muckraker" described a group of reform-minded journalists who published articles attacking human exploitation and corrupt institutions, intending to inform and engage the public. During their most active phase, between the years 1895 and 1910, muckrakers used popular magazines as their vehicles. Magazines such as *Collier's Weekly*, *Munsey's Magazine*, and *McClure's* had become popular amusement for the growing American middle class. *McClure's,* for example, provided political content and purposely targeted corporate monopolies and political machines. The muckrakers became household names across America after their articles appeared in the January 1903 issue of *McClure's. The History of Standard Oil,* by Ida M. Tarbell; *The Shame of Minneapolis,* by Lincoln Steffens, and *The Right to Work,* by Ray Stannard Baker, all appeared in that issue. Steffens had previously published the famous article, *Tweed Days in St. Louis,* comparing corruption in St. Louis with the Boss Tweed era in New York.

The problem of corruption in cities grew out of their extraordinary population growth and the unintended consequences of urban government structure. No one realized that municipal governments required a unique design, based on the need to respond quickly to the service needs of their citizens. Before 1850, America was a land of towns and villages, each using the same government that evolved during the original settling of the Colonies. By the late 19th Century, urban population growth had overwhelmed that model. In 1850, the ten largest cities in America had a combined population of 1.4 million. By 1890, that number was 6.6 million and by 1900, it was 9.4 million. When the States saw what was happening, they assumed their own model would work for large cities, so they set up city governments with two-house legislatures, administrative boards, and mayors as the executive. Those governments, besides being cumbersome, had no power because the States retained control of taxes, financing, and appointments to the administrative boards.

With an overly complex government and no administrative control, mayors realized they could not meet the needs of their constituents in a timely fashion, so they sought out political bosses for assistance. Those men were powerful politicians operating at the state level, who could influence legislation affecting the cities. Corruption followed quickly when a pay-for-favors system began to develop. The party bosses began to steer funds to the cities in return for city contracts, jobs for friends, or public franchises for their own corporations. History's most famous case is that of Boss Tweed, (William M. Tweed) who virtually controlled the government of New York City from 1863-1871.

Progressive action against urban corruption focused on ways for cities to generate their own revenue so they would rely less on the states and have money available to accommodate the changing needs of the public. Progressives proposed a system of municipal taxation, called single tax, whereby the cities would impose taxes on franchisees providing services, like water, sewer, and public transportation. In addition, the cities began taxing the property of the franchisees themselves. Those new sources of revenue allowed cities to operate an efficient service delivery system for the public.

Social Justice Advocates

On the social justice side, many dedicated individuals within the Progressive Movement worked tirelessly and on their own to make a difference for individuals. Jane Addams (1860-1935) was a social worker, political activist, and community organizer, who founded Hull House in Chicago in 1899. Hull House was a settlement house of the type pioneered in Britain. The concept was that volunteer, middle-class "settlement workers" would live among their low-income neighbors and share knowledge they could use to help mitigate their poverty. Settlement houses provided services such as daycare, education, and healthcare to improve the lives of the poor in those areas. Educational offerings included social, cultural, and intellectual programs and art classes for children. The houses also served as places to test social work theory, as well as stimulate intellectual discussions about the problems of society. Addams worked to enlarge the concept of civic duty so it included roles for women beyond motherhood; she believed women's lives should revolve around "responsibility, care, and obligation," as the source of women's power. She worked diligently on causes that were important to her, including a push to create a juvenile court system and laws that would limit women's workdays to eight hours. Addams was a charter member of the National Association for the Advancement of Colored People (NAACP) and received the Nobel Peace Prize in 1931.

William (W.E.B.) DuBois was an African-American sociologist, writer, and civil rights activist involved in the civil rights movement for almost seventy years, starting in 1894. DuBois received a PhD from Harvard and served on the faculty of Atlanta University. He was a cofounder of the NAACP, but was better known as the leader of the Niagara Movement, founded in 1905. The Niagara Movement was a group of African-American activists who campaigned for equal rights for blacks. They bitterly opposed the Atlanta Compromise, brokered by Booker T. Washington in 1895, which limited the rights of African-Americans in the South. DuBois, writing extensively, campaigned against lynching, Jim Crow laws, and discrimination. In his most famous book, *Black Reconstruction in America* (1935), DuBois showed that African-Americans were not responsible for the failure of Reconstruction. Convinced that Capitalism was the source of black inequality, DuBois joined the Socialist Party of America in 1911and continued to support the Socialist model of government for the rest of his life. After World War II, he was known to fraternize with Communist sympathizers, despite NAACP attempts to distance itself from that ideology, and he was forced to resign from the organization. Nevertheless, DuBois has been widely recognized for his pursuit of social justice for African-Americans and helping to set the stage for the freedoms they would achieve later.

Margaret H. Sanger was another of the energetic pioneers of Progressivism. Trained as a nurse, Margaret Higgins gave up her career when she married the architect William Sanger in 1902. When a fire destroyed their home on the Hudson River in 1911, the Sangers relocated to New York City. Margaret began working as a visiting nurse in the slums of the East Side and became interested in radical politics. She joined the Socialist Party, took part in labor actions of the IWW, and became friends with Socialist intellectuals like John Reed and Upton Sinclair. After seeing women die attempting self-induced abortions and noting the lack of information available about birth control, she decided to make it her mission to educate women on the subject so they would have more control over their own reproductive choices and functions.

At that time, The Comstock Law was in effect, which banned the sending of obscene material, including information about birth control, through the United States mail. In 1914, Sanger decided to push hard against that unjust law, launching a newsletter called *The Woman Rebel*, which focused on promoting birth control. Her goal was to challenge the Comstock Law in court, and the New York district attorney obliged by indicting her on obscenity charges later that year. Sanger fled the United States for Britain to avoid prosecution, but returned two years later. In October 1916, Sanger opened a clinic in Brooklyn for family planning and distribution of contraceptives. Police arrested her nine days later and charged her with operating a public nuisance. The court found her guilty and ordered her to spend thirty days in jail. At sentencing, the judge stated: "Women do not have the right to copulate with a feeling of security that there will be no resulting conception."[11] The conviction was overturned on appeal.

In 1921, Sanger started the American Birth Control League to educate American women about controlling the sizes of their families. Two years later, she opened the first birth control clinic, the Clinical Research Bureau, which eventually became Planned Parenthood. Sanger continued to write and speak about birth control for the rest of her life, living long enough to see a law passed legalizing birth control in the United States in 1972.

Theodore Roosevelt and the Progressive Movement

Theodore Roosevelt, a Republican, was the voice of the Progressive Movement during the first decade and a half of the 20th Century. A strong leader, Roosevelt was passionate about ending exploitation of the disadvantaged and curtailing the excesses of big businesses. Born wealthy in New York City, Roosevelt graduated from Harvard and attended law school at Columbia. He understood that wealth had freed him from class allegiances, but he retained a dislike for "moneyed men" because of their arrogant greed. Roosevelt was against both government by the mob and government by the rich, and saw himself as a new Federalist. He admired Hamilton but regretted Hamilton's view of Democracy. He understood Jefferson's view of the people but disagreed with his dislike of central government. Roosevelt believed a national government could only be effective if it was stronger than any private group in the country. He also believed the role of government was to protect the citizens against the unofficial power of business.

After the assassination of President William McKinley in 1901, Vice-President Roosevelt moved forward with his Progressive agenda. In 1903, he supported the passage of a law creating the Commerce and Labor departments. That year, he supported the bill creating a Bureau of Corporations with the power to investigate corporate business practices. He pushed through the Pure Food and Drug Law in (1905) and the railroad regulations act (Hepburn Act, 1906). Roosevelt was a champion of conservation and promoted the development of the National Parks System. With those accomplishments in place and the goodwill of the American people supporting him, Roosevelt made the biggest mistake of his political career. He honored a pledge not to run for President in 1908. Roosevelt's handpicked successor, William Howard Taft, won in a landslide but Taft lacked the skills to arbitrate a growing revolt within the Republican Party. The Conservatives and Progressives battled each other over the party philosophy, and both were disappointed by Taft's lack of support. It was not long before the frustrated Progressives abandoned the party.

As the election of 1912 approached, Roosevelt returned to the fold and attempted, without success, to unite the Progressives. The movement was just too fractured. The militant faction believed that only destroying special privilege and applying the rule of equity to all classes could save America. The moderate faction, supported by the likes of Roosevelt and Herbert Croly, wanted to pursue a more moderate program of Federal intervention and participation in economic and social affairs.

The Presidential Election of 1912 was historic, if for no other reason than its philosophical divide. Roosevelt ran for President as the Progressive candidate (Bull Moose Party); Taft ran as the Republican candidate; Eugene V. Debs represented the Socialist Party; and Woodrow Wilson ran as the Democratic candidate.

Wilson, the ex-president of Princeton, was only mildly Progressive because his roots were set in 19th Century laissez-faire capitalism and states' rights. He believed that government's role ended at the point of removing barriers to the full development of the individual. To Wilson, a more radical Progressive agenda was out of bounds. He campaigned on the plank that Roosevelt's promotion of social programs supported by his Progressives would lead to control of the Federal government by Big Business. Wilson advocated an alternative approach intended to destroy monopolies and stimulate business to revive competition. He won the election, defeating Roosevelt, with Taft a distant third. Debs, a lightning rod for citizens angry with their government, received almost a million votes.

New Progressive Intellectuals

In the first two decades of the 20th Century, a new group of Progressive thinkers emerged, including Herbert Croly, Walter Weyl, and Charles Beard. Croly (1869-1930), was co-founder of the *New Republic Magazine*, and the most important Progressive thinker of that period, after publishing his book, *The Promise of American Life* (1909). The Progressive philosophy had always embraced the Democratic Party's long-standing kinship with Thomas Jefferson, who founded it, but Croly broke with Jefferson, claiming he and Hamilton were both wrong about the ideal structure of government. Jefferson believed in small government and a strong Democracy controlled by the people. Hamilton was an elitist government proponent and believed control should be by the rich, for the rich. Croly believed those positions should combine into a new structure, combining a strong Democracy with a strong central government.

Croly's blending of Hamiltonian and Jeffersonian philosophies required rejection of Hamilton's arguments for institutional checks on a pure National Democracy, and Jefferson's arguments for limited government. Croly felt both were too closely tied to the Doctrine of Individual Rights. He wanted to transcend that doctrine to create a national political community. In his view, a strong central government needed strong individuals to lead it. His ideal was Abraham Lincoln, a person who understood that Democracy in America was a national ideal. Croly, like Hamilton, had faith in the powerful few and sincerely believed those few would remain Democratic. Civil libertarians who believed the powerful few would lead America to a totalitarian state challenged Croly's quest for a moral elite.

Croly firmly believed that labor unions were essential to creating economic benefit for the laboring class, and wanted unions to have the right to negotiate contracts for the employees they represented. Parting company with other Progressives, Croly did not want the government to fight large corporations. He wanted the Sherman Antitrust Act repealed and replaced with a National Incorporation Act that would regulate and nationalize corporations. Croly believed it was the responsibility of a powerful central government to practice "constructive discrimination" on behalf of the poor. His plan included a federal inheritance rate of twenty percent, rather than an individual income tax supported by other Progressives. Croly argued that compensation for work should be adjusted to the requirements of leading a normal life.

Walter Weyl (1873-1919), co-founder of the *New Republic* along with Croly, is best known for his book, *The New Democracy*, published in 1912. *The New Democracy* advocated the Democratic ideals of the Progressive movement, believing that comfortable material prosperity, would give Americans the opportunity to achieve greater social justice. He was against individualism, suggesting that collective action led by experts, by the state, and by national governments was the best way to improve society. Weyl thought the United States Constitution was too narrow and needed to be reworked from the standpoint of social justice. He believed progress required direct democracy; more regulation of big business; greater efficiency in business; and an increased role for labor unions.

Charles Beard (1874-1948), wrote, *An Economic Interpretation of the Constitution of the United States* (1913) and *An Economic Interpretation of Jeffersonian Democracy* (1915). To Beard, the Constitution was set up by rich bondholders in opposition to the middle class. He argued that the document was designed to undo the radical Democratic tendencies the Revolution created among the common people, especially farmers and debtors. Beard concluded the Constitution was built on a foundation of inequality, so the document must be corrected to restore the proper social order.

The Wilson Presidency

Woodrow Wilson directed his initial efforts at passage of the Federal Reserve Act of 1913, but remained distant from the Progressives as he moved forward with his own agenda. He opposed the AFL's attempts to expand its power;

opposed the child labor law; and worked against women's suffrage, believing the issue belonged to the States.

By 1916, the American political landscape had changed. The Progressives were soundly defeated in the 1914 elections, and there were rumors that Theodore Roosevelt would abandon his third party and rally the Progressives against Wilson. The President, in an historic pivot, adopted the Progressive agenda to save his political career. He started by naming Louis D. Brandeis to the Supreme Court in 1916. Brandeis was a renowned legal theorist who had entered Harvard Law School at age eighteen. He was a strong advocate for Progressive causes, known for fighting against monopolies and large corporations. Wilson worked to pass the Progressives' two pet issues of that time: child labor reform and worker's compensation. His newly adopted ideology got him enough votes to squeak out a victory over the Republican Charles Evans Hughes. After the election, political philosophies fell to secondary importance because the run up to World War I took center stage. The Progressive agenda was about to be put on hold.

The United States' entry into World War I followed a serpentine path. In 1915, Wilson decided that the United States could not let Britain fall to the Germans and he resented the immorality of the German submarine strategy. Unable to move forward because the United States had only a token standing army inadequate to fight a war, Wilson pressed Congress to authorize expansion of the army. Trying to avoid a Republican label as a pacifist, he pushed the bill forward until it passed in August 1916. Progressives demanded that the wealthy pay for the new army, so Congress obediently passed tax increases to cover the debt. The debate became more complicated when Wilson asked Congress for the authority to arm American merchant ships. Congress saw that as an undeclared war against the Germans and refused to move forward. The debate became moot when German U-boats sank three American merchant ships on March 16, 1917. Wilson asked Congress to declare war on April 2, thereby moving America into the European conflict.

Socialism and WW I

The Socialists in America met harsh political opposition when they opposed American entry into World War I and tried to interfere with the conscription laws that required all younger men to register for the draft. After war was declared, the Socialists began holding rallies against the War, calling it an immoral crime. Two months later, President Wilson signed into law the Espionage Act, which included a clause providing prison sentences for up to twenty years for "Whoever, when the United States is at war, shall willfully cause or attempt to cause insubordination, disloyalty, mutiny, or refusal of duty... or willfully obstruct the recruiting or enlistment of service of the United States."[12] During WWI, about half the Socialists supported it; the other half were under attack for obstructing the draft. On September 5, 1917, at the request of President Wilson, the Justice Department conducted a raid on the IWW. They stormed every one of the forty-eight IWW headquarters in the country. By month's end, a Federal grand jury had indicted nearly two hundred IWW leaders on charges of sedition and espionage under the Espionage Act. Their sentences ranged from a few months to ten years in prison.

Just eighteen months later, the War was over. In the interim, the United States had equipped an army, deployed it to France, sold bonds to help cover the cost of the war, and retooled industry to produce the ships, planes, and bullets needed to win. Victory was complete, but the peace

117

terms accompanying it would put the United States in a difficult position. The League to Enforce Peace, a task force appointed by Wilson and chaired by former President William Howard Taft, developed Wilson's peace plan, called the Fourteen Points. The plan sought to create world peace based on shared future interests, not vindictiveness. It supported the creation of a League of Nations, a partnership of goodwill between countries, a preview of the concept that would later become the United Nations. Strongly supported by the Progressives, Wilson's plan created an opportunity for America to influence world politics for the better.

Unfortunately, America's allies were not in a mood to be idealistic and were far more determined to settle the score with Germany. The Allies rejected Wilson's plan and the League moved forward without the United States. Back home, Congress rejected the Versailles Peace Treaty because it contained a provision that could draw the United States into war without the approval of Congress. After many attempts at compromise, Congress passed its own resolution repealing acts of war against the Axis Powers and reserving American rights under the Versailles Treaty. Wilson unsuccessfully vetoed the bill. Rather than become a partner in European politics, the United States decided it was more comfortable retreating into Isolationism.

The period of 1918-1920, was one of tremendous turmoil. First, World War I ended in November of 1918, so the United States had to transition back to a peace time economy. Second, a devastating two-year worldwide Influenza pandemic began and ultimately killed 500,000 in the United States. Finally, union problems boiled over as soon as the war ended, and the first "Red Scare" occurred in 1919.

The United Mine Workers (UMW) under John L. Lewis called a strike for November 1, 1919 in all soft coal fields. They had agreed to a wage agreement to run until the end of World War I and now sought to make permanent their wartime gains. Attorney General A. Mitchell Palmer invoked the Smith-Lever Act (1914), a wartime measure that made it a crime to interfere with the production or transportation of necessities. Ignoring the court order, 400,000 coal workers walked out of the mines and pits. The coal operators played the "Radical" card, saying Lenin and Trotsky had ordered the strike and were financing it. Some members of the press reiterated that language.

The "Red Scare" appeared during the midst of the union turmoil. Terrorist plots were uncovered and some attacks succeeded, causing mass hysteria and irrational reactions to the perceived Communist threat. Against that backdrop, the American electorate decided it wanted change. The Republicans looked over a list of undistinguished candidates and selected Warren G. Harding because he was controllable by party bosses. The result was a Harding landslide. His scandal-ridden administration ended after two years when he died of a stroke. Harding was among the worst Presidents, burdened with an administration rocked by scandal.

CHAPTER TEN

PROGRESSIVE MOVEMENT 1920-1945

Freedom has more often been lost in small steps by progressive incrementalism, than it has been by catastrophic upheavals such as violence or war.

James Madison

The 1920s heralded a sea change in the attitude of the American public. The combination of the reform effort, WWI, economic instability, and the Red Scare was too much for people to take, so they decided to have fun instead. The sexual revolution began as women broke out of their traditional roles. Aside from gaining a means to travel at will, owning an automobile was a new indicator of increased social status. Ignoring Prohibition, men and women sought places to drink together and have fun. There was a significant explosion of music, specifically Jazz, and there was an evolution of dance, including the scandalous Tango. New entertainment venues appeared with motion pictures and radio. It was a time of rapid and fundamental social change.

The Socialist Movement

After Lenin's successful revolution in Russia, he invited the American Socialist Party to join the Third International in 1920. The debate over whether to align with the Soviet Union caused a major rift in the ASP. A referendum to join Lenin passed with 90% approval, but the moderates who were in charge expelled the extreme leftists before the conference. The expelled members formed the Communist Labor Party and the Communist Party of America. The Socialist Party, with only moderates left, shrank to one third of its original size. The Communists organized the Trade Union Unity League to compete with the AFL and claimed to represent 50,000 workers.

The Socialists had lost a major ally in the IWW, and their free speech had been restricted, if not denied. Immigrants, a major base of the Socialist movement, were discriminated against and looked down upon. Eugene Debs, leader of the Socialists, was in prison, along with hundreds of fellow dissenters. Wilson's National War Labor Board and numerous legislative acts had reduced the plight of the workers; they began to be less interested in radical activities. The Socialists were regarded as a dangerous group of untrustworthy radicals. The press, courts, and other establishment structures railed against them. Strikes were beaten down by force, and the economy was doing well enough to get public sentiment on the side of the corporations and the government but against the unions.

The World Communist Party's Fifteenth Party Congress was held in Moscow in 1927. During that meeting, the overthrow of capitalism around the world was a primary topic. This time was labeled the Third Period and all Communist sympathizers were urged to help make the world revolution a reality. The stock market crash of 1929 seemed to support that reality, but things changed permanently because of two events: the election of Franklin D. Roosevelt as President of the United States in 1932 and Adolf Hitler's rise to power in Germany in 1933.

Roosevelt's election and the passage of the National Industrial Recovery Act in 1933 sparked a tremendous upsurge in union organizing in 1933 and 1934. Those new members were less interested in agitation because they were now receiving the benefits of union membership. Many conservatives equated The New Deal with Socialism or Communism, and saw its policies as evidence that the government had been heavily influenced by Communist policy-makers in the Roosevelt administration. Marxian economist Richard D. Wolff argued that Socialist and Communist parties, along with organized labor, played a collective role in pushing through New Deal legislation, while conservative opponents of the New Deal coordinated an effort to single out and destroy them as a result.

Conservative Reaction

Beneath the layer of freedom and fun that characterized the 1920s, fires of discord began to burn brightly. Two major currents started wreaking havoc on the American society. The first was a reaction against change and a call for the return to traditional values; that perspective set up a battle between traditional values and scientific materialism. The second was the intellectual unrest and repudiation of Democracy.

The combination of a rapidly changing society and the horrific experience of WWI made Americans feel life was out of control, so they sought a return to a more structured morality. Prohibition was passed in 1919, over Wilson's veto, as an attempt to apply morality to behaviors many felt were sinful. It was an idealistic effort, and one of many attempts to use legislation to solve social problems. During WWI, there had been a ban on alcohol to conserve grain but various groups, including pious Protestants and the Anti-Saloon League pushed to make the ban permanent, once the WWI ended. History undeniably records the unintended consequences of the Eighteenth Amendment. Crimes associated with bootlegging and illegal manufacture of liquor were rampant, there was a loss of tax revenue, and there was a wholesale flaunting of the law.

Darwin's theory of Evolution was another target for the conservatives. Within many churches and denominations, the notion that man could have evolved from other creatures and was not placed on earth by God was heresy, if not anathema. Early in the decade, new laws appeared specifically to block the teaching of evolution in schools. The impetus for this was pressure applied by religious leaders who felt the naturalist philosophy was trying to replace the moral foundation of religion. Three states made teaching evolution a crime subject to imprisonment, while debates on the subject were undertaken in twenty-three more states. By late in the 1920s this issue of evolution took a back seat to other, more serious problems.

Nativism

The most lethal Conservative attack against the frivolity and lack of morality of the 1920s came from those espousing a Nativist philosophy. Nativists believed that society must aggressively protect its people against outsiders. The movement began with an active crusade against immigration but that crusade quickly expanded beyond its original scope. Those with more radical fundamentals preached intolerance of minority groups, stating they were too unfit or impure to be part of American society. The most potent of the antagonists was the Ku Klux Klan (KKK), which re-emerged in 1915. The KKK grew to some five million members by 1925 and continued, their hatred for Catholics, Jews, and anyone else who was not a patriot for American purity. The Klan focused its attention on bigotry, violence, and corruption, and its vengeance had no boundaries. It was successful at infiltrating some state legislatures and influencing policy, but the immoral and illegal approach to patriotism would eventually turn the American people against it. External opposition and infighting led to a collapse of the movement by the end of the 1920s, as its membership dropped to thirty thousand. Even with its loss of prestige, the Klan remained as a threatening specter in the South and would rise again later.

Intellectual Trends across America

The second set of major currents at work during the 1920s was intellectual unrest and repudiation of Democracy. The Progressives were deeply disappointed with the results of their commitment to the Democratic cause, laid out to the world through Wilson's Fourteen Points. Rejection of the American plan meant a continuation of world politics as usual. Wilson's attempt to carry the Progressive program to the world had failed, and the outcome of the treaty fight at home was just more of the same. Progressives were also unhappy to see the same governmental authority that protected the people before the War, now denying them basic rights. Between Prohibition, the anti-evolution crusade, and Nativist groups like the Ku Klux Klan, it seemed like America was supporting a complete reversal of all the Progressives had accomplished in the prior decades.

The Progressives had become cynical about the innate virtue of people and their place in the Democratic ideal, which offered equal opportunity for everyone. They also expressed indifference to a middle class unable to meet its own needs. A segment of the Progressive intellectual leadership felt they were at war with the middle class, and all the crusades for its benefit and all the talk about moral idealism had been wasted. Progressives began to highlight individuality rather than class goals. In their revised version of morality, they turned up their noses at the low culture of the masses. Some repudiated Democracy as a political system and applauded the Soviet system as the ideal. In effect, the young intellectuals did not like the society in which they found themselves. They hated the anti-intellectualism of small towns, the demand for conformity, and the emphasis on the utilitarian virtue of benevolence. Those attitudes persisted for most of the "Roaring Twenties", before fading as 1930 approached.

The Coolidge Presidency

Although the work of the Progressive movement continued during the administrations of Harding and Calvin Coolidge, fractionalization and its connection to the Democratic Party hampered it progress. A brief Depression in 1921-22, caused great discontent in the Midwest and led to a call for a Conference for Progressive Political Action to be held in Chicago in 1922. The purpose of the conference was to determine whether the Progressives should take independent political action or rely on the traditional parties to fix the economy. They decided to wait to form a third party until after the 1922 elections were complete, believing the outcome would give them a better gauge on the mood of the country. The results were encouraging, so another conference was scheduled for December 1922. The

Progressives decided Robert La Follette should campaign for the Republican nomination for President and, if that failed, he would launch a third party. The Progressives knew they could be beaten by a Democrat who embraced their platform, but it turned out that the Democrats were too fractured to pose a threat. Insurgent Republicans tried to sell the campaign of La Follette to the elites of their party but got nowhere, so the Progressives formed their own party and nominated La Follette. The Republican, Calvin Coolidge, won by a landslide and the Progressives were back to square one.

Coolidge, who had been Harding's Vice President, took office in 1923 and served until 1929. He followed a pro-business policy with little attempt at business oversight. Progressive efforts continued at the state and local levels, where the delivery of social services was most important. The Progressives waited patiently for the right opportunity to emerge and Wall Street delivered it on a silver platter when the stock market crashed in 1929. The Crash was the result of excess, unregulated speculation on the part of investors who were convinced the market could never go down. The resulting economic disaster lasted for nearly a decade and caused immeasurable harm to the American economy and its people. President Hoover, slow to respond to the crisis, was largely blamed for the debacle.

Progressive Thinkers

John Dewey (1859-1952) is considered the most important American Progressive thinker during the first half of the 20th Century. Dewey, most recognized by his work in educational reform, held political views that were equally important. He attacked classical Liberalism as being too focused on the individual and neglectful of account for the relationship between individuals, which is the real structure of society. While classical Liberals looked at freedom as the absence of external constraints, Dewey asserted that freedom was "the positive act of participation in an ethically desirable social order".[13] Dewey was also anti-elitist because he distrusted the intentions of those in power. He believed Democracy had to have active participation of the electorate so as to guarantee freedom. He criticized Liberals for not treating people as individuals. Freedom, in his view, was not only relief of constraints against the individual, it also had to empower the individual.

John Maynard Keynes (1883-1946) was an economist who debunked classical economic theory and favored a more Progressive form, which would more fairly protect all social classes. Opposing the classical views of supply-side economics, Keynes advocated a mixed economy in which the private sector was dominant but the government took a key role during recessions. Keynes asserted that unemployment resulted from imbalances in demand, depending on whether the economy was expanding or contracting. During periods of economic contraction, there was no guarantee that manufactured goods would be purchased, so unemployment resulted when companies cut back on production. To counter this phenomenon, it was necessary for the government to use deficit spending to stimulate the economy and accelerate the country along the business cycle. He wrote, "For Government borrowing of one kind or another is nature's remedy, so to speak, for preventing business losses from being, in so severe a slump as to present one, so great as to bring production altogether to a standstill."[14]

Keynesians rejected the idea of a balanced government budget because its impact would encourage saving, reduce demand for products, and raise unemployment. The preferred solution was to offer tax cuts as an additional tool to stimulate the economy. They also believed adding profits during boom cycles and taking away profits and income during downturns exaggerated the cycle by making it more extreme at each end. Keynes had a profound impact on American economic thought from the time of the Great Depression through the 1960s. Franklin Roosevelt employed Keynes' economic principles during the Depression and they were prominent in management of the American economy during the post war period starting in 1945.

Franklin Roosevelt

Frustrated and alarmed at the economic crisis following the stock market crash, the American people turned to Franklin D. Roosevelt and elected him by a landslide in 1932. Roosevelt will forever be associated with his New Deal, which, on the surface, appeared to be a bottomless basket of comprehensive social programs that would help pull the United States out of the Great Depression. The real story is much more complicated. There were, in fact, two New Deals; the first, from 1933-35, was a period of cautious Progressivism; the second, from 1935-39, demonstrated a full embrace of Progressive principles. During the first period, all classes and special interests demanded action and were united in their points of view. Then, in 1935, conservative and business interests abandoned the coalition, forcing Roosevelt to build a new alliance to move his programs forward. With the advent of the Second New Deal in 1935, corporations broke with President Roosevelt and unions took their place as a strong ally. Socialism was dead and Communism survived only through its presence in the unions. The Communists now supported the New Deal as necessary to oppose Fascism. Roosevelt did not anticipate assuming the role of Progressive champion but political forces moved him in that direction.

The first step Roosevelt took after his election was to restore confidence in the American financial system; he ordered a four-day bank holiday beginning March 4, 1933. The Economy Act of March 20, 1933 followed and not only drastically reduced government expenditures but also moved the government toward a balanced budget. While troubled banks were re-organizing, new laws were passed to prevent speculation. Homeowners were helped by the creation of the Homeowners Loan Corporation (1933) and the Federal Housing Authority (1934); the former to help homeowners in trouble and the latter to help people buy homes and stimulate home construction. Roosevelt's second step was protecting the American farmer; the Agricultural Adjustment Act (1933) realigned and stabilized supply and demand.

In May 1933, the Administration announced the National Industrial Recovery Act, one of the most pretentious and idealistic pieces of legislation ever conceived. It featured a full, planned economy managed by bureaucrats, who would determine manufacturing production levels, the length of the work week, and employee pay rates. Each industry would have its own code, with instructions on how to operate their businesses. It took two years to create the first codes, but by that time, business leaders realized that this new plan would severely hamper their ability to operate. Fortunately, the Supreme Court declared the law unconstitutional in 1935.

During the first years of the Roosevelt Administration, popular opinion became polarized as the public moved Left and Right from the center of the political spectrum. Disadvantaged groups on the Left, including the unemployed, destitute, and aged, began applying pressure on the Administration to create innovative programs to help them; in 1934, the midterm election sent that message to Congress. Between 1934 and 1936, the Works Progress Administration (1935); The Rural Electrification Act (1936); and the National Youth Administration (1935) were created in response. The crown jewel of that period was passage of The Social Security Act (1937) that created a system of retirement benefits for all working Americans.

Modern Liberalism Formed

Liberalism was originally an Enlightenment term that originated in Europe. Sometimes called Classical Liberalism for the sake of clarity, it defined the political philosophy of limited government, laissez-faire economics, and unalienable individual rights, intended to replace the titled class structure of old Europe. Liberalism in the Unites States is not the same thing and, for that reason, has been has been more specifically described as Modern or Social Liberalism.

As mentioned previously, one of the first objectives of the Progressive Movement was to counter laissez-faire capitalism and Social Darwinism theory. That effort immediately separated it from European definition. As their work evolved, Progressives saw big government as the engine needed to achieve their goals, so they moved even farther from the European idea.

The Second New Deal

There was no Liberal movement in the United States prior to the presidency of Franklin D. Roosevelt. Starting in 1935, the New Deal coalition shifted as business leaders, unhappy with the National Industrial Recovery Act, withdrew their support for the President. The labor movement stepped in and began to press the federal government to create programs to assist the unemployed. At the same time, Roosevelt was forced to respond to disgruntled reformers and demagogues representing sharecroppers, subsistence farmers, and the indigent poor, who had not benefited from the New Deal. Sensing a change in the political winds, Roosevelt accepted responsibility for assisting those groups and put in motion a new set of programs that included deficit spending, redistribution of wealth, and social legislation.

This "Second New Deal" departed from traditional Progressive theory in its shift in attitude toward business. Government would no longer endeavor to break up trusts and interfere with a free business environment: it would now allow business to operate freely and regulate it in a way that avoided stifling economic growth. That system of regulation became reality with the Social Security Act and the Wagner Act, which strengthened the hand of labor unions in their negotiations with business.

Roosevelt was elected again in 1936 and his campaign that year was marked by two shifts in the electorate. The first was the strong alliance of labor and the Democratic Party, cemented by labor's efforts on behalf of the President. The second shift saw African-Americans abandon the Republican Party and vote Democratic for the first time.

Not all Roosevelt's ideas were acceptable to the American people, however. In 1936, Roosevelt became frustrated with the Supreme Court because it found too many of his new initiatives unconstitutional. To alleviate that problem, he introduced a bill that would allow him to appoint one federal judge for each existing judge who did not retire six months after reaching the age of seventy. Fifty appointments would be permitted under this plan, including six on the Supreme Court. That would allow Roosevelt to pack the Court and make sure his programs were approved. This attempt to democratize the judicial branch was seen by Congress as an attempt to create a Presidential dictatorship, and it was defeated by the combined efforts of both parties.

In response to unwarranted fear of an economic collapse in 1937, the Roosevelt Administration tightened controls on banks; which threw the entire country into a recession and forced Congress to act quickly to minimize the damage. With the approach of war in 1939, the Progressive agenda was put on hold as the country's attention moved to the debate about America's isolationism in the changing world. Roosevelt would be elected again in 1940 and 1944 to become the first president to server more than two terms. The pivotal election for him was 1940. He was thinking about running but knew if he was elected he would break Washington's unwritten rule about a two-term limit. Roosevelt made the decision to run when he would not find a worthy successor to carry on his programs. In 1944, the war was moving to a climax and Roosevelt did not think it appropriate to transition the government during a time of national crisis.

The death of Franklin Roosevelt and the end of World War II marked a significant turning point in American history. The Depression was over, America had won the war and the United States had a new role as superpower on the World Stage. The battle continued between Democrats who wanted to carry forward the Progressive banner and Republicans who resisted what they saw as an intrusive government.

The accomplishments of the Progressives during the Roosevelt years were a demonstration of the expansion of Progressive ideology throughout the American political system. Progressive intellectuals had come back to the fold, and ready to push new programs forward. Social scientists conducted new research into previously unsolvable problems and laid bare many of the unpleasant but undeniable facts of American life. Their focus on issues like The South, the concept of region, the plight of African-Americans, and poverty sought to set the stage for a healthy reconstruction. Economists embraced principles of the Keynesian economic theory as they sought to arm the government with the tools needed to manage the economy. Progressive intellectuals expanded the horizons of Democratic ideology, assuming the New Deal institutional system was sound and did not need radical transformation. They came to believe they could accomplish more by agitating for social justice, rather than merely engaging in politics.

CHAPTER ELEVEN

HISTORY OF THE PROGRESSIVE MOVEMENT 1945-2000

There are two ways to conquer and enslave a country. One is by the sword. The other is by debt.

John Adams

Harry Truman, vice-President, assumed the Presidency upon Roosevelt's death in April 1945. Truman came with a plan to continue a Progressive agenda, but Congress had split into factions, so developing a consensus for legislation would prove difficult. The Democrats were struggling with civil rights, labor policy, and inflation. The Republicans had their own controversy, as internationalists argued with isolationists, ignoring the need to develop a rational domestic policy.

Truman supported the Murray Bill (November 1945), which set up the Council of Economic Advisors and America's second attempt at a planned economy, but he was at odds with Republicans and some Democrats regarding the continuation of a full Progressive slate. A fight over the Price Control Bill (vetoed June 1946) led to inflation that year and precipitated a Republican landslide in the Congressional elections. As a counterforce, the Republicans pushed through the Taft-Hartley Act (restraints on trade unions) over the President's veto in 1947.

Nominated for President in his own right in 1948, Truman faced Thomas Dewey, Governor of New York, who was the Republican Party's nominee. Campaigning hard and shrewdly maneuvering the Republicans into appearing indecisive, Truman eked out a narrow victory.

Liberal-Progressive Split

During the Truman administration, the fusion of Progressive and Liberal philosophies broke apart over Communism. Anti-Communist liberals, led by Walter Reuther and Hubert Humphrey, expelled the far-Left from The New Deal Coalition, and committed the Democratic Party to a strong Cold War advocacy. Those Liberals were committed to the quantitative goal of economic growth that accepted large, near-monopolies, such as General Motors and AT&T, while rejecting the Progressives' dream of the structural transformation of government. In addition, Liberals endorsed a balance of power between labor and management, an expansion of New Deal era social welfare programs, and an embrace of Keynesian economics.

Progressives reacted against this trend in 1948 by forming their own party and nominating Henry Wallace as their Presidential candidate. Wallace carried forward the traditional Progressive philosophy by supporting further New Deal reforms, stronger control over big business, and opposition to the Cold War. The Communist Party endorsed Wallace, but his reluctance to disavow that endorsement damaged his campaign and he finished fourth in the Presidential race. Liberals were now in firm control of the American political narrative and the Progressives were on the sidelines. The Liberalism takeover of the American political narrative had been so quick that, by 1950, Lionel Trilling would write, "In the United States at this time Liberalism is not only the dominant but even the sole intellectual tradition. For it is the plain fact that nowadays there are no conservative or reactionary ideas in general circulation."[15]

Truman's Second Term

With Democratic majorities in Congress again in 1948, Truman pushed forward a new set of programs called The Fair Deal. He achieved some victories with amendments to the Fair Labor Standards Act (1949), and Social Security Act, but failed to win a national health insurance bill. Progress in civil rights was completely blocked by the Southern states. Ultimately, the tide turned against President Truman when the Korean War reminded Americans about the threat of Communism. Public anger intensified when the Alger Hiss case implied the Roosevelt and Truman Administrations were too cozy with Communists and tolerated their positions in American government.

Truman's Progressive Fair Deal was built on a New Deal foundation, but was different enough to warrant a separate identity. It rejected Communism and committed the United States to an activist foreign policy, a significant break from the country's tradition of isolationism. The Fair Deal was also suspicious of excessive concentrations of government power.

Eisenhower

By 1952, the public lost faith and grew tired of the Truman Administration and the Korean War. The President chose not to run for a second full term. The timing was perfect for the Republican Party because America wanted a President who could rise above politics and be cautious and moderate in dealing with the new world order. Dwight Eisenhower was elected by a landslide in 1952 because he fit the mold the public was seeking. Progressivism was on hiatus. A powerful Liberal-union coalition had formed in Congress, but the Republican majority limited its effectiveness. That cancelled out Liberal efforts to develop new programs. The high hopes expressed for the new President during the 1952 campaign were not realized. After Eisenhower dealt with the perceived Communist threat and the associated McCarthy scandal, the government became gridlocked. Breaking up The New Deal coalition left a vacuum in policy on both sides of the political aisle, leaving the country with no clear path forward.

Meanwhile, public voting patterns had changed with a large swing segment of Americans who voted a "split ticket." The Progressives' path back to relevancy was limited by their own success, as the previous generation's farmers and city workers joined the middle class and became more independent. In the South, two factions rose to power: segregationists and business elements, both of which were parts of the emerging "New South." Both opposed the traditional Democratic Party; both would become part of a new GOP coalition in the region.

The net result of the Eisenhower years was a middle-of-the-road approach, which made all constituencies unhappy. Eisenhower did seek a modest expansion of New Deal economic and social policies but those issues generated resistance among Republicans who wanted to keep the status quo, and Democrats who thought the President needed to do more, to go farther. Despite his general disagreement with Congress, Eisenhower pushed through an Education Bill (1956) and the Civil Rights Act (1957), which expanded voting rights for African-Americans.

Civil Rights Movement

The Eisenhower years marked the beginning of a new phase of the Civil Rights movement, as the Federal government, African-American activists, and traditionalists from the South collided. Momentum for that progress was based on simple history. When African-Americans moved north to escape segregation, they found themselves stuck in large cities, without opportunities for jobs and with little control over their lives. That led to an activism for equality that northern politicians could not ignore, so they began to move forward on civil rights. The Democrats of the "solid South" held the power to control civil rights legislation and blocked all progress there. The Democratic Party came to realize that progress in civil rights would require a new coalition that excluded the South. That would mean a loss of the South to the Republicans, so they would have to rebuild their coalition to stay in power. They accepted that reality.

The first great step forward occurred with the Brown vs Board of Education Supreme Court ruling of 1954, which held that segregation was unconstitutional. Thurgood Marshall, who later became the first African-American Supreme Court Justice, argued the case. In 1955, two events occurred that affected Civil Rights. The Emmett Till case involved the murder of a fourteen-year-old African-American boy who was visiting family in Mississippi. Allegedly, he whistled at a white woman. Those accused of his murder were acquitted but later bragged they did kill him. That kind of injustice ignited efforts to achieve African-American equality. Later that year, in Montgomery, Alabama, Rosa Parks was arrested for refusing to give up her seat on a bus to a white man. That event precipitated a bus boycott in Montgomery that lasted a year and ended bus segregation.

In 1957, there was a confrontation at Central High School in Little Rock, Arkansas when officials attempted to integrate the school. On orders from Arkansas Governor Orval Faubus, nine African-American students were blocked from entering the school. President Eisenhower sent in Federal troops and the National Guard to intervene on behalf of the students. A Federal judge blocked the Governor from further action to prevent integration.

Kennedy-Johnson

John Kennedy was elected President in 1960, and Americans hoped his New Frontier would ignite another, better period of prosperity. Kennedy sincerely believed in civil rights and the plight of African Americans, but many other problems forced his attention elsewhere: the Cuban Missile Crisis; the emerging and enlarging problem of continued conflict in South Viet Nam; and the ongoing Cold War. Kennedy, a Liberal, accomplished some Progressive agenda programs, including expanding unemployment benefits, raising the minimum wage, and passage of the Equal Pay Act (1963), which was intended to eliminate wage disparity based on gender.

After the assassination of Kennedy in 1963, it fell upon the shoulders of Lyndon Johnson to carry out Kennedy's domestic agenda, as well as his own. Johnson idolized his mentor, Franklin Roosevelt, and hoped to complete Roosevelt's New Deal agenda. LBJ's Great Society gave the country Medicare; the Housing and Urban Development Act; the Education Act; and the Civil Rights Act, all passed in 1965.

Progressive Action

Although the Liberal philosophy was in control of the American political narrative during that period, many Liberal priorities overlapped those of the Progressives. The Johnson Administration enacted the greatest number of Progressive programs since the time of Franklin Roosevelt. His team crafted a revised version of social and economic justice that was greatly influenced by Keynesian economic theory. Under that version, the assumption was that massive public expenditure would speed economic growth, and provide public resources to fund larger welfare, housing, health, and educational programs. Johnson's policies lacked any hint of radicalism and there was little disposition to revive New Deal era efforts to concentrate economic power. There was no intention to fan class passions or redistribute wealth, all of which were departures from classical Progressive thought.

Student Revolt and the New Left

In the late 1950s and early 1960s, American colleges and universities experienced a surge in enrollment causing them to increase their faculties and invest in campus expansion. Their policies, however, were very restrictive toward students. The universities saw themselves acting as "baby sitters" for the students while they were on campus. That eventually caused a pushback reaction, which began with

141

the free speech movement at the University of California - Berkeley in 1964. After protests, some of which were violent, the Berkeley faculty sided with the students against the university administration. Students took lessons from the civil rights movement, including grass roots organizing and defiance of authority.

The student movement accelerated when the Viet Nam War added to the cause. Starting in 1965, there were protests across college campuses and protest organization like the Students for a Democratic Society (SDS) came into being. Tension rose to a fever pitch in 1968 when students at Columbia University occupied two administration buildings. The movement gradually grew into protests against American Society and became known as "The New Left," a phrase coined by American sociologist C. Wright Mills. The New Left was critical of large bureaucratic organizations such as big business, the military, and universities. The SDS, using the traditional Progressive position written in its Portland Statement (1962), called for an end to foreign intervention.

Fall of Johnson

Lyndon Johnson fell prey to the global interventionist rules he inherited from the post-World War II period. President Kennedy sent the first advisors to Viet Nam as the beginning of an effort to control Communist expansion in the Far East. In mid-1964, faced with a major decision, Johnson decided that withdrawing from Viet Nam was not an option; instead, he chose to escalate the conflict. In August 1964, the Gulf of Tonkin Resolution passed in Congress giving Johnson full approval to further accelerate the long-term war. By the end of 1965, there were 190,000 American troops in Viet Nam. By 1967, that number was

500,000. In 1968, the North Vietnamese launched 100 coordinated surprise attacks on South Vietnamese cities known as the Tet Offensive; the attacks occurred on the day of the Vietnamese Tet, or New Year celebration. The accomplishments of that offensive gave a psychological boost to North Viet Nam and turned America against the war.

In March 1968, Johnson announced that he would not run for President that year. He made his decision based on polling that showed the Democratic Party was so divided, he could not have obtained the support he would need to win. Expansion of the Viet Nam War and the acrimonious divisiveness it caused across America, not only brought down Johnson, but also put Progressive progress on hold once more.

Nixon Elected

The chaos of 1968, which featured a bitterly divided Democratic Party and bad blood between the New Left and the Liberals, essentially gave Richard Nixon the presidency. While he rhetorically attacked Liberals, in practice he pursued some Progressive policies. Nixon established the Environmental Protection Agency by executive order; expanded the National Endowment for the Arts and Humanities; began Affirmative Action policies; and opened diplomatic relations with Communist China.

In 1973, Nixon withdrew all American combat troops from Viet Nam and signed a peace treaty to end that war. He also eliminated the Draft. Despite some left-leaning programs, Liberals and Progressives hated Nixon and rejoiced when the Watergate scandal forced his resignation in 1974.

Progressive Intellectual Thought

John Rawls (1921-2002) stands out as perhaps the greatest moral thinker in the history of the Progressive movement and one of the most important philosophers of the 20th Century. He created a new path for social contract theory, earning himself a position as the darling of the 21st Century Progressive Movement.

Rawls built his philosophy upon a modern version of social contract foundations from which he created a theoretical model of society. He coined the term, "veil of ignorance," to describe how and why individuals choose the kind of society they want, without knowing what physical or mental capabilities they'd have in that society. For example, if people did not know their gender in advance, they would choose to live in a gender-neutral society. Likewise, if a person did not know how intelligent he would be, he would choose a society that was fair to all, regardless of intelligence. Applying that process to all human life would result in a political model that was the most socially just for America. Rawls asserted that the world consisted of human beings who possessed various characteristics and were influenced by varied factors. If individuals could make moral decisions neutral to most parties, those irrational factors that influenced them would not come into play. This would lead to an "ends justify the means" argument because individuals would be distributing rights without knowing what was and was not good.

Departing from the utilitarian gospel, Rawls believed that political systems should work to benefit the least advantaged in society, rather than all of society. To make that work he defined a hierarchical distribution system for primary social goods. At the top level were liberties (rights); at the middle level were opportunities; and at the third level were income and wealth. When individuals built a government, and encountered conflict between social goods, the choice was based on the hierarchy. For example, if one were evaluating affirmative action (a right) against college student acceptance criteria (an opportunity), the right would have a higher priority. Rawls' theory was used in the college entrance quota system that was popular in the latter part of the 20th Century. The quota system denied rights to non-minority students and was later overturned.

Rawls saw rights as they were written in the Constitution, but viewed opportunities as vehicles for obtaining equality. In other words, opportunities would provide the greatest good to the least advantaged and to open all offices and positions to everyone. He viewed income and wealth through the lens of his "difference principle," meaning that distributive justice had to first be applied to the least advantaged. Rawls placed an important qualifier on programs designed to help the disadvantaged; they could tolerate inequality so long as they achieved their purposes.

Rawls' value to moral philosophy was rooted in two concepts. First, his theory suggested a way for philosophy to remove itself from the unsolvable moral dilemmas that have plagued it for centuries. Second, he focused on the moral arbitrariness of human beings to show that, in the absence of absolute morality, there must be a rational system to guide the relationship between human beings in modern society. If people accept the need for distributed justice, then it must lead to the redistribution of wealth. Those whose property would be taken had to accept the loss of the satisfaction and motivation that were part of acquiring and owning it. Rawls easily fit into the Progressive model because his views sought to overcome inequality to create equal opportunity. He opposed the inequality of Capitalism and the ideas of Social Darwinists, who endorsed differences in talent as the measure of where an individual should end up in life.

Ford and Carter

Vice-President Gerald Ford replaced Nixon as President of the United States, but his two short years in office were ineffective. Suffering scorn for his pardoning of Nixon, Ford fought uphill against large Democratic majorities in Congress. When a recession began in 1975, Ford's fate was sealed, and he was beaten by Jimmy Carter in the 1976 election. Carter took power in a troubled time and was forced into crisis mode. He pushed for a national energy policy to try to contain the exploding oil crisis, but it took two years for the bill to make its way through Congress. After negotiations, the bill was watered down and lacked some of its key benefits. At the same time, interest rates rose to stratospheric levels because of energy costs and inflation. Carter had some foreign policy successes, such as the Camp David Accords (1978), a peace treaty between Israel and Egypt, but the Revolution in Iran and the taking of American hostages in Teheran, was a crisis Carter was unable to resolve. The six years of Ford-Carter were nearly devoid of any Progressive programs or accomplishments.

Reagan and G. H. Bush

In 1980, Ronald Reagan defeated Jimmy Carter and ushered in the most notable change to American political philosophy since the New Deal. Reagan was a bona fide Conservative, who awoke a Conservative tide in the country that propelled him to victory. The Republican Right, out of power since the 1930s, was united in its opposition to New Deal Liberalism and post-1960s Federal power in civil rights, education and criminal justice. The Republican Right also opposed the further secularization of American life and the erosion of the status of the American family. It expressed hostility toward any compromise with the Soviet Union.

Reagan's accomplishments were substantial, both in foreign relations and in domestic policy. He helped set the stage for the fall of the Soviet Union and, at home, presided over one of the largest economic expansions in American history.

When Reagan reached the end of his second term in 1988, George H.W. Bush was nominated for President, and he won in a landslide over Michael Dukakis. Bush, labeled as the legitimate heir to Reagan, was distrusted by Conservative purists because of his lack of pedigree. Frustrated by disagreements with a majority Democratic Congress, Bush spent most of his time on foreign affairs, most notably presiding over the fall of the Berlin Wall. When he went back on his pledge not to raise taxes, it contributed to his defeat by Bill Clinton in 1992.

The Reagan-Bush years were a continuation of lean times for the Progressives. Their political influence had been eclipsed since 1950, and they continued to work toward an opportunity in the future. The New Left had created momentum for change as an alternative to the failed Liberal agenda, but the Progressives could not take advantage of this opportunity because they were too disorganized. They needed a spark to rally around. That spark would come sixteen years later with the Obama presidency.

Bill Clinton

The election of Bill Clinton, in 1992, broke the twelve-year run of Conservative power in Washington. Clinton won by adopting the "Third Way" political philosophy advanced by Stephen Skowronek. That approach sought to "undermine the opposition by borrowing policies from it to seize the middle and achieve political dominance" (Stephen Skowronek, The Politics Presidents Make, 1993). Third Way adherents embraced fiscal conservatism to a greater extent than traditional social Liberals; they advocated some replacement of welfare with workfare; they espoused a strong preference for market solutions to traditional problems; and they rejected pure laissez-faire economics and libertarian positions.

The Presidency of Bill Clinton provided another interesting sidetrack in the history of the Progressive Movement. Clinton had great instincts as a politician and they kept him in office longer than any Democratic president since Franklin Roosevelt. Overcoming setbacks from his first term, like the failure of comprehensive health care legislation and the loss of control of Congress in 1994, Clinton reinvented himself as a Centrist and was elected comfortably to a second term.

In practice, he was not a Progressive but he ignored that ideology to stay in power. Clinton apologists try to point to some Progressive accomplishments by him, but it is clear there was not a lot to say. Holding up the Brady Bill or the Health Insurance Portability and Accountability Act as great accomplishments made for a weak resume. The Clinton years were an aberration in the sense that the Centrist positions taken by Clinton did not alter the Left/Right power balance. Progressives who claim it was a betrayal of Left wing ideology have heavily criticized his approach.

CHAPTER TWELVE

PROGRESSIVES IN THE TWENTY FIRST-CENTURY

*I am for doing good to the poor, but I differ in opinion
about the means.*

*I think the best way of doing good to the poor is not making
them easy in poverty, but leading or driving them out of it.*

Benjamin Franklin

The Progressive Movement has exerted influence on
American politics in varying degrees since 1870. Most
often, its influence was related to its relationship with the
political party controlling the White House. Occasionally,
Progressive ideology ran counter to the trends of the time,
causing it to be marginalized. A list of the ebbs and flows
of Progressive influence looks like this:

- 1870-1910 Initial phase of the Progressive
  Movement

- 1910-1920 Marginalized over opposition to
  World War I

- 1920-1930 Marginalized by Republican
  presidents and the 20s mindset

- 1930-1945 In power as a partner in New Deal programs

- 1945-1960 Marginalized over America anti-communist foreign policy

- 1960-1968 A partner with Liberals in Johnson's Great Society

- 1968-1980 Marginalized by Republican presidents and Liberals but re-energized as the New Left by opposing the Viet Nam War

- 1980-1992 Marginalized by the Reagan-Bush presidencies

- 1992-2000 Limited power due to the Clinton Ideology

Twice, the Progressives were marginalized over foreign policy, opposition to World War I, and opposition to the Truman Cold War doctrine. Between 1950 and 1980, the Liberals, who controlled the Democratic Party, marginalized them once again. After 1980, Liberalism was discredited but the Progressives did not reestablish their position until the Obama election, twenty-eight years later.

During the period from the New Deal until the mid-60s, Liberalism expanded to include the middle class, international trade, and government spending with the aim of maintaining full employment. That required a significant increase in the size of the Federal government, and was effective until Johnson's Great Society and the Viet Nam War years. At that point, Liberalism began to break into two factions. One faction was, "...the subdominant, who are joined by the shared goal of seeking haven from market pressures, as well as insulation from majoritarian moral and social norms often seen as discriminatory. The alliance includes 1) the victims of economic competition – low wages workers, the unemployed, and the unemployable – without the skills to prevail in the postindustrial economy, 2) racial, ethnic, and other minorities, historically barred from social and economic participation, and 3) those seeking support in the aftermath of the cultural revolutions of the past forty years that have led to divorce and extramarital birth rates which leave single women and children in need of the basic necessities of life."[16] Those groups have always been targets for Progressive help.

The second faction was, "made up of highly educated voters, frequently in professions the require advanced degrees. Over the past four decades, the conversion of professionals (variously known as "knowledge class", "new class", "information workers", or "symbol analysts") to a solid base for the Democrats has helped compensate in numbers for the defection of skilled and semi-skilled lower income white workers to the Republican Party."[17]

The Elitist Faction

From 1960 to 2000, the percentage of Democratic voters in the professions increased from 18% to 35%, while the percentage of skilled and unskilled workers dropped from 50% to 35%. The elitist faction does not vote Democratic to improve their economic condition, like the workers from the 1930s did. They follow the traditional Progressive line opposing business interests as greedy and exploitive. Their core focus is in the areas of rights related to self-expression, such as self-development and individualism. They want government to support programs that match their ideology and rights that express a modern view of social justice, like gay rights, women's rights, or the freedom of self-expression. They are openly hostile to any expressions of traditional morality, such as those of the Christian Right.

That faction was built out of the affluence of the late 20th Century and victories obtained along the way, such as forcing the end of the Viet Nam War and bringing environmental issues to the attention of government. Today's Progressive elitists exert influence through their ability to support the party financially, but they are very different from the party's other constituencies, who are more conservative. Where the elitists see the Republican Party as a threat to personal freedom, middle and lower income white voters are attracted to its comforting moral and religious belief systems.

That conflict limits the Progressive's opportunity for success, because every Presidential election cycle requires messaging to try to draw middle class whites back into the coalition.

George W. Bush and Barack Obama

The George Bush Presidency, at its outset, created an opportunity for renewal of Progressive action. Elected by the smallest margin in history, Bush's victory caused a lot of anger among those on the Left who felt Al Gore was cheated out of the Presidency. They soon expanded their ranks after the large tax cuts of 2001, which benefited the wealthy more than anyone else.

The decision that defined the Bush presidency more than anything else was the war in Iraq in 2003, in response to the Terrorist Attacks of 9/11/2001. Foreign interventionism had always been opposed by the Progressives and, in that case, the situation was made worse by the discovery that no weapons of mass destruction existed in Iraq. Of course, the war continued much longer than expected, claimed more American lives than anticipated, and cost more money than it should have. Before and during the time of the Iraq War, Progressives launched protests nationwide. According to Alex Callinicos of *The Socialist Worker* of March 19, 2005, between January 3 and April 12, 2003, for example, 36 million people in the United States and around the world took part in almost 3,000 anti-war protests. Anger over the war eventually reached beyond the Progressives, to include the majority of Americans. When the revenge factor wore off, Americans started to see the conflicts in Iraq and Afghanistan as a mini-Viet Nam. All the questions about Bush were punctuated by the severe economic downturn of 2007, which destroyed Bush's poll numbers and opened the door for a Democratic victory in 2008.

The following quote from a contributor to the *Daily KOS* in 2008, describes 21st Century Progressive thinking the year Obama was elected,

> Here we are today, in what I believe is the beginning of the post-post liberal era... Two things become clear. First, there is a space that will open in American politics for new agendas, fresh approaches, and new thinking. Second, the consequences of which ideas we will choose are very high. Will we take up the banner of liberalism, and strive valiantly to repair the damage that has been done, and to try once more the make the system we have more livable for the American people...Or do we instead take up the banner of Progressivism, and attempt to construct a new way of life, ...knowing as we do that the one we have now is dangerously blind to human need? [18]

Barack Obama was elected, then re-elected to the Presidency, based on his personal charisma and the inability of the Republican Party to put together a competitive message. Obama's accomplishments followed a traditional Progressive line.

- Passed the Affordable Care Act

- Passed Wall Street Reform (Dodd-Frank)

- Ended the war in Iraq

- Repealed "Don't ask don't tell" for gays in the military

- Boosted fuel efficiency standards

- Created conditions to close the dirtiest power plants

- Revised pay equity laws

- Signed the Food Safety Modernization Act

- Expanded wilderness and watershed protection

- Passed the Fair Sentencing Act

- Crafted next generation school tests

As one would expect, those accomplishments did not satisfy Progressives who criticized Obama for not going far enough. Criticisms were leveled at him for too much foreign intervention, letting Wall Street off the hook after the damage it did to American mortgage holders, and a lack of effort in advancing environmental and social issues.

Donald Trump

The election of Donald Trump has turned American politics on its head and has driven the Progressives to distraction. Some would say Trump's victory was set up by Obama's close relationship with Wall Street, the nerve center of the Capitalist oligarchy. That helped make Trump the outsider, even though he is a New York businessman. Trump succeeded, in part, because the Democratic Party discarded white lower- to middle-income class men, who saw themselves excluded by the party in favor of minority groups. Trump used a Populist playbook and appealed to groups that had been disaffected for a long time. His election was no accident. As shocked as the Progressives were about the reality of the 2016 outcome, there is clearly a set of lessons here. For most of the election cycle, Progressives linked the message with the personality of the messenger and that fooled them into believing the message would not get through.

New Progressive Playbook Needed

The challenge Progressives face today is how to apply an anachronistic ideology. To be successful and move forward, they must overcome five obstacles. Without a new plan, they face a long winter ahead.

First, the position of the Progressives on the American political spectrum has changed. In 1905, a significant percentage of Progressives were members of the Republican Party, having been attracted to the philosophy and force of will of Theodore Roosevelt, the first President to openly support Progressive goals. Progressives abandoned the Republicans during the Wilson years and never looked back, having found a more comfortable home in the Democratic Party. The Democratic Party that operated from 1912 until the New Deal Era was very different from the version that exists today. Before the mid-1930s, there was no Liberal faction. It came into existence under Franklin Roosevelt and controlled the direction of the Democratic Party for thirty years, before falling out of favor. Today Progressives must coexist in the Democratic Party with newly cast Liberals, who share many of the same objectives.

Second, the Progressives have accomplished so much in the past, that there is less for them to do now. That is not to say exploitation and unfairness have been removed from America, but the residual pain impacts smaller groups than before. In the initial period of Progressive action, there was exploitation of large groups -- farmers, racial minorities, union workers and others. Today's constituencies are smaller. For example, African-Americans are 13% of the population so the size of their constituency and their capacity to lead efforts on their own behalf are less than that of larger groups.

Third, Progressives have less influence within government than they did a hundred years ago. Their efforts are now offset by groups of equal and opposing power and views. Those groups include members of their own party, as well as members of the Right. To make things even more difficult, Congress is fragmented and party differences have become much more nuanced.

Fourth, American culture has changed. We live in a time of greater sensitivity to the plight of the disadvantaged and there are more organizations ready to assist and render aid.

In addition, the number of government programs available to help those in need is substantially greater than ever before, so the cry for help is not as loud.

Fifth, the Progressives themselves have changed. Their elitist faction does not have the same political interests as the rest of the Democratic Party, so the party has internal conflict it needs to resolve. This makes it more difficult to build a unifying message that can win elections.

The Progressive Gene carries on its work today, pushing the Left to seek their lofty goals on a very complex and challenging playing field. David Schultz offered the following explanation:

> The progressive politics that appears dead is that of Lyndon Johnson, John Kennedy, Franklin Roosevelt, and even Teddy Roosevelt...It is about the spirit of John Rawls, Michael Harrington, and Dorothy Day and a commitment to believing that the government has an essential role in make sure we are a nation that is not one-third ill-fed, ill-clothed, and ill-housed, that kids should not go off to school hungry, and that corporations should not have the same rights as people. [19]

Shultz went on to criticize Democrats for not having the will to fight. They consistently give in to Republican threats and do not stand up for their constituents. He believes that positive action cannot take place as long as the Progressives are tied to the Democratic Party, so they must ultimately break away. He admires the Republican Tea Party example and would like to see the Progressives move in that direction. Democrats are the self-appointed caretakers of government, but their need to be responsible is outweighed by their lack of courage in the face of possible government shutdown.

The Republicans can easily exploit the Democrats' unrest; between the two parties is a political contest of who will blink first. Progressives are essentially on political life-support because their ideals are muddled within the Democratic Party.

CHAPTER THIRTEEN

PROGRESSIVE IDEALISM

Every form of addiction is bad, no matter whether the narcotic be alcohol or morphine or idealism.

Carl Jung

The Progressive Gene powers the moral center of the Progressive philosophy and is a specific result of collective human evolution. Those with the Gene are driven to exercise their outsized caring and fairness morality toward a Utopian view of government as an agent working for its people. Progressives attack cold, uncaring Capitalism because they perceive it as a corrupt cultural construct that promotes social and economic inequality. In their eyes, the Capitalist system is repressive, prejudicial, and ineffective; it must be discarded. The caring and fairness morality of the Progressives is the foundation on which a caring, fair government should be constructed. If this goal were achieved, inequality would be gone forever.

History does not look fondly on similar attempts to replace Capitalism. The Utopian political philosophy of Communism was a failure. Socialism, more akin to the aspirations of Liberalism and the welfare state, also failed. Accepting those failures as bumps in the road, the Progressives have embraced a different path: changing the American Constitution so that it supports the construction of a welfare state. The process of achieving that task has moved forward, step-by-step, over time.

Progressives have always had a strong belief system that defines how government should operate. Their zeal for change ignites their idealized view of their government's capability to build and manage a political system in which inequality no longer exists. They insist that a Socialist or pseudo-Socialist system can succeed, despite its never working before. The theories of Marx were grossly flawed, misunderstood, incorrectly applied, and Utopian. Everyone was fooled when Lenin proved successful at leading the revolution in Russia that produced a Communist state, but the resulting political system was a sham. It was an autocracy in Communist clothing.

Still, the Progressives yearn for a Utopia, the Edenesque world where the economic playing field is level for all people. To that end, they work tirelessly to employ science as a tool to manage government efficiently and direct it toward ensuring the benefits of those who need help. Government comes with bureaucracy and the inherent inefficiencies of its structure, so there will always be a gap between the goals of a law and the government's ability to deliver results that match those goals.

Progressives as Utopians

Utopian beliefs and experiments predated the Progressive Movement. Two thousand years ago, Plato proposed a Utopian government in his dialog, *The Republic*. Fifteen centuries later, Thomas More described a Utopian society in the New World, which was a perfect welfare state. As previously discussed, Fournier and Owens tried to build Utopian communities but they were unsuccessful. Those failures did not deter the early socialist thinkers who continued to cling to the utopian ideology as the basis of their political system.

> The Utopians' mode of thought has for a long time influenced the Socialist ideas of the 19th Century, and still governs some of them. Until very recently, French and English Socialists paid homage to it. The earlier German Communism, including that of Weitling, was of the same school. To all those, Socialism was and is the expression of absolute truth, reason and justice; once discovered, truth, reason and justice will conquer the world by virtue of its own power.[20]

The first Progressive intellectuals in the United States also embraced Utopian ideals in their desire to overcome the abuses of Capitalism. They viewed property as evil, so the only way to avoid its corrupting influence was through public ownership. As much as the Progressives wanted a Utopian model to succeed, they were never able to make it happen despite two hundred years of trying.

Utopian beliefs remain today in the hearts and minds of many Progressives. For example, a 2009 article written for the *Daily KOS,* stated:

> The problem, here, is not that Progressives are 'utopian' in the unrealistic sense of the term. Progressives do not need to be any more "realistic" than they already are -- the history of Progressive politics under neo-liberalism reveal as much. Of course, they don't want to live in a fantasy world either – but we do little justice to our problems if
> we trivialize the activity of utopian dreaming. Utopian dreaming has an important purpose. Utopian dreaming reminds us to ask for

more...[P]rogressivism does not go far enough in its critique of this world, nor in its suggestion of how to build a better one."[21]

Has Utopian ideology merely been wishful thinking by the Progressives, or does it offer a viable alternative to the Capitalist model?

Progressive View of Science

Progressives have long looked to science as a tool to fix the problems of society. Economics has always been their favorite subject. The other social sciences, like sociology and psychology, became established at the same time, but political influence by practitioners and experts in those disciplines had to wait to express themselves until the welfare state got underway.

The idea that economists could advise government on the degree of state intervention in markets was based on the Progressives' belief in the moral authority of science and its ability to explain the behavior of the American economy. In his book, *The Scholar's Duty to the State* (1878), John Bates Clark argued that using economics to understand the causes of poverty was more valuable than charity. Economists, once believing in the American ideal of individualism, began to favor a government-based economy. That shift was a sign of the times, based on four influencing factors: European sociology; the Protestant Church's effort to bring the kingdom of God to earth; the liberalizing effects of Pragmatism; and the idea of an American hierarchy that was group-based, not individual-based.

Progressives developed the idea of the modern administrative state, which would subordinate the amateurism of politicians to expert advisers working as members of a professional civil service. In his popular eugenics text, Albert Wiggam stated: "Government and social control are [now] in the hands of expert politicians who have power, instead of expert technologists who have wisdom. There should be technologists in control of every field of human need and desire"[22]

In his book, *Social Control* (1901), Edwin Ross advocated a system of controls which, like education, would be charged with the shaping of individual minds. He reasoned that human beings were nothing more than "plastic lumps of human dough" which needed to be formed on a social kneading board. Frederick Taylor's book, *The Principles of Scientific Management* (1911), treated human behavior at work as a science, promising fairness in the workplace and the transfer of workplace control from the corporation to technocrats; the belief was the application of scientific analysis would produce both fair working conditions and efficiency. *The New Republic*, commenting on the obsolescence of the *Bill of Rights* stated, "What inalienable right has the individual, against the community that made him and supports him?"[23]

The Progressives belief in the moral authority of science was the foundation of this effort. For example, biology could control human genetics (eugenics) and genetics, properly managed, could guide economic progress. The operation of this model required "expert" managers who would be trusted to remain disinterested while they worked to manipulate workers and produce a fair, efficient, economy. John R. Commons (1862-1945), reflecting on those trends in the 1930s, stated, "Progressivism is a theory of social progress by means of personality controlled [programs], liberated, and expanded by collective action. It's not individualism, its institutionalized personality."[24]

Progressives use for Government

By 1910, the Progressive Party had achieved some of its fundamental goals and members looked forward to advancing their agenda for America. That agenda required an intellectual foundation that would redefine traditional American beliefs: embracing government as a change agent rather than an adversary; attacking the sanctity of the Constitution with its focus on private property; and fostering the notion that society as a whole was more important than the individual. That point of view helped establish the Progressive goal of building a powerful, centralized state, in which government would serve as the means to achieve social good.

Government had two major roles in the implementation of the Progressive agenda. The first was using the courts to remove the Constitution's focus on individual rights in favor of the rights of the groups. The second was the creation of the institutions required to implement the agenda. Those institutions would utilize academic research to design programs to protect and improve the lives of Americans. The resulting programs would operate through government departments which would monitor and manage them.

Government Comes with a Bureaucracy

Former presidential candidate Eugene McCarthy made the following statement about bureaucracies, "The only thing that saves us from the bureaucracy is inefficiency. An efficient bureaucracy is the greatest threat to liberty."[25]

All who have been frustrated by the process of interacting with government bureaucracy would agree with his statement. On second look, however, McCarthy's statement has two interesting insights. First, bureaucracy and inefficiency were partners. The architecture of a Capitalist bureaucracy was antithetical to human behavior, because human life allowed for unstructured behavior and moment-to-moment adaptation. Bureaucracy could not accommodate either of these behaviors. Second, McCarthy identified bureaucracy as the greatest threat to liberty. His point was that bureaucracies were created by law but, when implemented, separated themselves from the people's ability to control them.

Politicians do not manage a bureaucracy, it manages itself. To the extent that bureaucracies become oppressive, they take control away from the public. The conduit for citizen complaints about government is through their elected officials, but in trying to control bureaucracies, elected officials lack authority and are powerless.

Private enterprises have a primary goal of making a profit, so a company's sole purpose is to increase revenue and minimize cost while delivering its products to the market. Companies operating at a loss must either return to profit or cease doing business when their debts become unmanageable. Ultimately, the success of profit-seeking enterprises comes from the acceptance and demand for its products in the marketplace. The proof for this is that many people are willing to pay for it. Using the profit-motive as a guide, free enterprise adjusts its operations to the desires of its customers. The desire for profit pushes every entrepreneur to provide services the consumers deem most important.

In contrast, public enterprises operate without regard to profits; consequently, the level of satisfaction of its clients is not a measure of its value. Structures like the IRS or Federal Trade Commission (FTC) measure efficiency by number of tasks completed or number of clients served, without a measurement of the quality of that service.

In a bureaucracy, "success" is total and thorough execution of the rules of the operations manual. Because public services have no price in the market, management tools from private enterprises have no use; scientific management or time studies are unrelated and have no application. Bureaucracies use a centralized administration and restrict the freedom of their workers to ensure overall efficiency. Since any worker's performance cannot be assessed through efficiency, the safest way to prevent excesses and the abuse of power is to ensure everyone adheres to the same organizational directives.

Max Weber, the pioneer of sociological analysis of bureaucracies, believed that the late 19th Century bureaucratic model was a consequence of the Modern Era; it was designed according to rational principles that provided efficient service delivery to their clients. In Weber's view, bureaucracies were essential to make large scale planning for the state and its economy possible. They also allow heads of state to mobilize and centralize their resources of political power. Weber also noted the problems inherent in a bureaucratic structure. Its repetitious processes made it unwieldy and inflexible, and have a depersonalizing effect on individual bureaucrats. Furthermore, depersonalization has a spiraling effect and causes bureaucrats to focus more and more on process and less on service to their clients.

Weber's notion of bureaucratic alienation was similar to that of Marx; both identified the alienation of industrial workers and both saw alienation as negative. Weber, however, disagreed with Marx that alienation would eventually lead to revolution. Weber saw future bureaucracies as controlling man in ways he could not escape, but instead would have to live with.

The most prolific researcher on bureaucracies was Robert Merton, who wrote the seminal book on bureaucracies, *Social Theory and Social Structure* (1957). Merton agreed with Weber, but went beyond him to highlight and discuss the problems of bureaucracies. Merton coined the term, "unintended consequences" to describe the inefficiencies that developed in those organizations over time. Bureaucracies are created with a clear link between the actions of their workers and the achievement of their goals. In other words, the ends justified the means, so if the goals of the organization are not met, the bureaucracy fails.

Merton suggested that the operating rules of the bureaucracy appeal to individuals with a rigid personality type who can become obsessed with procedural compliance. Those individuals believe in rigid conformity with rules, regardless of whether they benefit the goals of the organization or the satisfaction of its clients. If rules become more important than results, the organization will take on ritualistic behaviors. Pressure applied by the bureaucracy on its staff creates sentiments that are overly intense and lead to a transference of focus from the goals of the organization to its rules. This leads to rigidity and failure to adapt to changes, which ultimately conflict with the goals of the organization. Since bureaucratic roles have a graded career structure, conformity becomes a part of a worker's operating philosophy. This leads to a sanctification process in which staff and workers develop an attitude of moral legitimacy for their work, independent from the organization.

In a bureaucracy, according to Merton, individual behavior becomes group behavior, through common sharing of the same destiny, namely a long-term career. Group members share interests because the career structure eliminates the need for competition and in-group aggression is minimized. Although group behavior benefits the organization, it can also lead to members working together to defend the group's self-interest and acting against the goals of the organization. If, for example, the group decides an incoming manager does not adequately recognize its status, it might sabotage the manager's efforts.

Members of a bureaucracy feel pressure to depersonalize their relationships with clients because the rules of the organization take precedence over non-standard problems a client may have. That conflict causes friction during client interactions. In the private sector, a client can complain on the grounds of customer dissatisfaction, but that is not possible in a bureaucracy. In fact, there can be negative implications within the organization when staff members appear to be "too personal" in their dealings with clients. Those individuals may be ostracized by the rest of the group; or removed from the organization, strengthening the cohesion of the remaining group. Issues that result from worker behavior add to the problems that inherently exist in bureaucracies.

The New Judicial Reality

In the past, Progressives could frame legal action broadly based on a substantive view of social and economic rights. The courts, reaching outside the Constitution, used those cases to sanction new positive rights, making the federal government guarantor of those rights through the welfare state. Today, that approach no longer works, because the courts are refusing hand down decisions supportive of this long used Progressive strategy. Moreover, the Congress and the Executive branch have now joined the courts in that opposition.

Changing strategy, the Progressives now take a more utilitarian approach to equality arguing that rights should be defined in a way that produces the same result for all. Along the way, they also have come to realize that achieving equality through the courts can be problematic because of unanticipated threats to other important moral values, such as liberty and democracy. Using this concept of equality widens popular appeal, broadens the coalition supporting the initiative, and increases its chance of success.

The Progressives have also changed their tactical focus. They use state courts when they are more helpful and leverage global opinions to strengthen their efforts. Some states are willing to extend rights beyond limits set by the federal judiciary, and those would-be candidates for Progressive action. Globalism becomes a conduit to Progressive action when the issue in question has global implications. For example, global warming is an issue that reverberates across the globe, so utilizing foreign interest groups to apply pressure in favor of domestic efforts increases the leverage.

This new "asking for less" strategy creates a balancing act for the Progressives: the success rate may improve but the successes are smaller. Ultimately, they will have to decide how their Utopian ideology must be reconciled with the scale of their results.

The New Government Reality

Progressives have come to recognize the problems that accompany big government are inefficiency and waste.

That realization has fostered a recent growth in "civil society" efforts. Some Progressives now see collective community efforts as a substitute for conventional political action between the state and the market, between sovereign political action and individual self-interest. Civil Society initiatives combine the characteristics of entrepreneurship, voluntarism, and civil mindedness, all of which are practical compared to impractical welfare state programs. Over the past two decades, Civil Society efforts have generated many experimental programs that have been supported by philanthropic organizations and educational institutions. Civil Society advocates assert that with Progressives' efforts at the national level stalled, much is being accomplished at the local level. Others warn that exaggerating the significance of these programs is dangerous if they suggest they are a substitute for real federal government action.

CHAPTER FOURTEEN

GRADING ECONOMIC PROGRESS

The welfare state is the oldest con game in the world. First you take people's money away quietly, and then you give some of it back to them flamboyantly.

Thomas Sowell

A brief analysis of relevant economic data supplies the answer to this question: Are Americans better off because of the efforts of the Progressives? To do the analysis correctly, the data must represent metrics often seen by the public and used by the Progressives themselves. As always, there is a cautionary note here: depending on their interpretation, the same statistics may support different points of view. It is consistency and correlation of data over time that provides cohesive trends.

The data selected for this evaluation have been assembled into the ten charts listed below

- Growth of government employees

- Growth of government spending

- Growth of entitlement spending

- Change in percent of income for the top 1% of incomes

- Change in the income ($) of American families

- Change in the wealth of the top 1% of wealthy

- Change in the wealth ($) of American families

- Change in poverty rate over time

- Comparing government spending, income, wealth, and poverty rate in one chart

- Historical income in the US for three time periods.

Growth of the American government has been, and is relentless, especially in the decades since the New Deal Era. Progressives see government as the panacea for society's ills; growth is good from their point of view. Entitlements are very large portion of government spending and should be examined separately because there has never been an easy way to control their expansion.

After government growth, household income and household wealth give a sense of financial well-being; household income shows how well a family can meet daily financial obligations; household wealth shows how well a family can deal with emergencies and retirement. Poverty, the fourth metric, is the most important of all. People who cannot afford housing, clothing, and food are the most disadvantaged and have the greatest need. It is a universal goal of today's political systems to provide support for individuals suffering the most.

Growth of the Government Employees and Spending

The growth in government employees has been substantial over the last sixty years. Starting in the New Deal years, the number of federal employees expanded and then leveled off starting in the 1950s. (See Chart 1). In 1955, the year state and local government data were added to the chart, there were about 14.5 million government employees in Federal State and local governments. In the latest year shown (2010), the number is 31.5 million, or a 217% increase.

The employee numbers for the Federal government appear constant over time and seem to indicate the growth of Federal workers is under control. That is false, because of a huge increase in the numbers of government workers hired as Federal contractors. They are not counted as Federal employees and act as a "shadow workforce." The growth in in Federal contractor expenditures, between 2000 and 2012, was 111%; the total cost for the Department of Defense contractors for 2012 only was $ 361 billion, and the total cost for non-defense agency contractors was $ 156 billion.

Along with the growth in federal employees, there has been significant growth in federal spending during the century between 1913 and 2013. (See Chart 2). There was a spike during World War II but then, starting in the 1950s, there has been an accelerating increase in expenditures. For example, expenditures in 2013 were eight times higher than those of 1953.

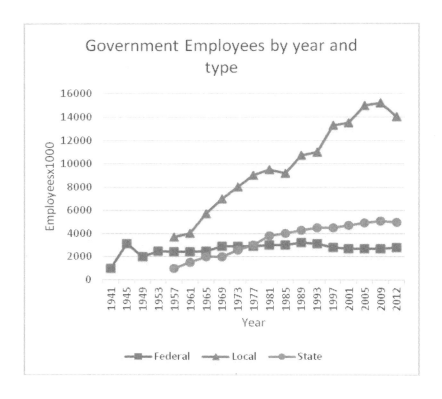

Chart 1 Source of data: Bureau of Labor Statistics 2012

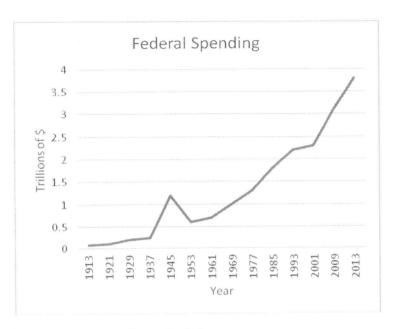

Chart 2 Source: LibertyInsight.com

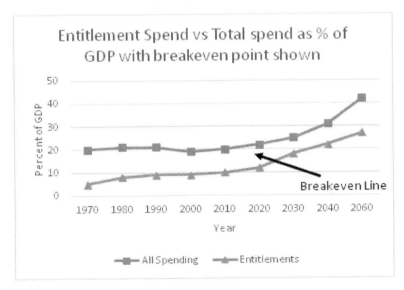

Chart 3 Source: GAO Citizens Guide, 2007

Entitlement Spending

Entitlement spending refers to programs that deliver services to the people who regard those services as their right. Entitlement is a clear goal of Progressive welfare state but only becomes possible through enactment of laws. Entitlement budgets, unlike other government programs, cannot be reduced. Entitlements include Social Security, Medicare, and Medicaid.

Based on the level of entitlement spending currently, if there is no reduction, government entitlement expenditures will exceed Federal income sometime between the years 2030-2040. (See chart 3). Moving forward into the future, the federal government will incur increasing deficits that will create risks for economic stability. There will be a reckoning when it is no longer possible to kick the can down the road.

Income

The percentage of total US income held by individuals earning the top 1% of incomes by year gives a measure of economic inequality across the nation. (See chart 4) The share of total income held by the top 1% is constant over time. If you examine the ends of the graph; it was 18% in 1913; and 21% in 2013. In the 40-year span from 1943-1983, there is a long parabolic curve where inequality drops after World War II and then rises again. The trend toward greater inequality, starting in 1980, is used by the Progressives as evidence of a return to the Gilded Age of haves and have nots, but it's fair to say the reason for the rise is not totally clear. Thomas Piketty (July 2001) has suggested that the current gap reflects a retrenchment of the labor force away from manufacturing and toward an

Information Age economy. New businesses achieve high-income levels before the professions that support them have matured.

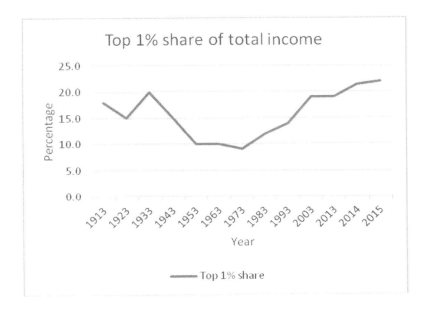

Chart 4 Source: Saenz, E. (2016)

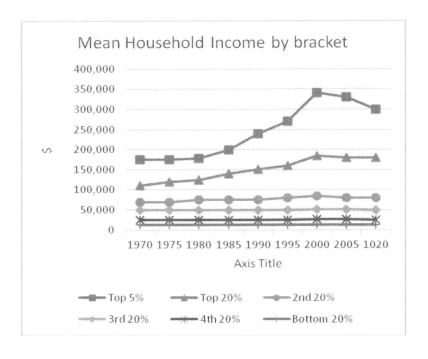

Chart 5 Source: US Census Bureau, 2015

The average income for Americans can be conveniently divided into six groups (See chart 5): the top 5% and the five 20% fractions of the total. The top 5% has an average income of $ 320,000, the top 20% has an average income of $ 180,000, and the bottom 20% has an average income of $ 10,000. Higher income groups have benefited from increased income over time, while the lower end groups have seen little benefit. A recent study published by the Congressional Budget Office (CBO) in December 2016 cites four reasons for the increasing income gap, which has been growing since 1985.

- Labor income has become unequal because some factors have tended to curb wage growth of lower- and middle-income workers relative to higher income workers. These factors include technological change, globalization, declining unionization, and minimum wage fluctuations.

- Other changes aided by globalization and technological change, such as economies of scale, winner-takes-all markets, and the superstar phenomenon may have boosted wages for very high-wage workers. Change in pay dynamics and social norms may help explain the rise in CEO pay.

- The distribution of financial wealth has grown more unequal over time, which affects income inequality through the capital income that wealth generates.

- The changing demographic composition of households has also contributed to income distribution patterns. Over time, there has been an increase in two earner households, single headed households, and marriages between couples with similar earnings or educational attainment.[26]

Wealth gives an indication of family security, because wealth protects against emergencies and provides comfort in retirement. Wealth also contributes to income in the form of return on investments, so the wealthy have additional income not available to those who live solely on employment income. (See chart 6)

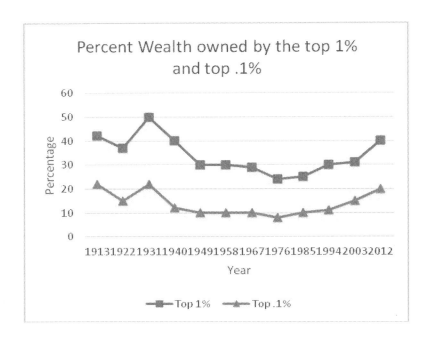

Chart 6 Source: Saez, E (2016)

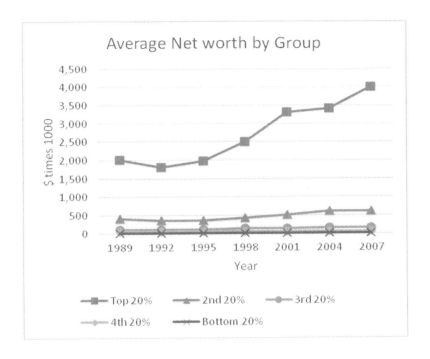

Chart 7 Source: US Census Bureau, 2015

The percentage of wealth controlled by the top 1%, is essentially the same as it was 100 years ago – 44% in 1913; 41% in 2012. The changes in between are similar to the income data. There was a drop during and after World War II, followed by a plateau period, and then a rise to the current day. This is not surprising because wealth and income are interrelated. High income creates extra money for investments that produces wealth. Part of wealth shows up as income when returns on investments are realized. The other important factor to consider is the built-in advantage the wealthy have. They have more money to invest so their return at a given interest rate is proportionately greater. One million dollars at 4% interest is $ 40,000 returned. One thousand dollars at 4% interest is $ 40!

Net worth over time, as shown by 20% fractions of the population, is similar to income. (See chart 7) The top 20%, enjoying the advantages discussed above, can compound their returns faster than those with lower net worth.

Regarding income and wealth in the United States, the relationships among different economic classes have not changed significantly over time. There are fluctuations, and most recently, there have been trends toward inequality. Despite everything the government has done to alleviate imbalances in economic opportunity, it has accomplished nothing that we can see in these metrics.

Poverty is a universal consequence of large human societies, which did not exist in man's primitive egalitarian state. Causes of poverty are historically due to lack of income, some inability to function in society, or isolation from those who can help. (See chart 8)

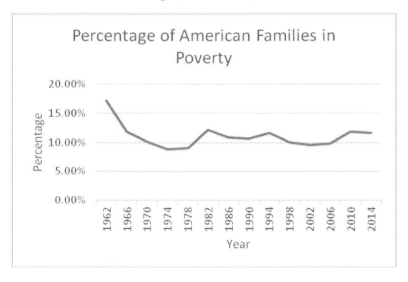

Chart 8 Source: US Census Bureau 2015

Since 1970, there has been virtually no change in the poverty rate. This is another case where the welfare state has failed to deliver.

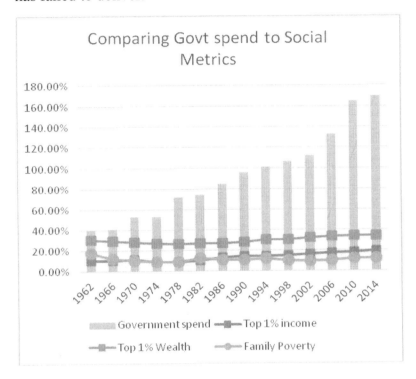

Chart 9 Source – Various listed above

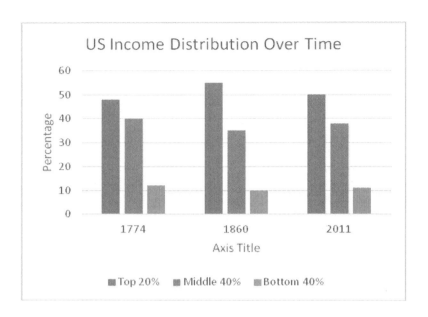

US Income Distribution Over Time

Chart 10 Source: World Economic Forum (2016)

Combining all the previous metrics into one chart creates the relationship between them easy to see. (See chart 9) That chart clearly shows that Federal expenditures have grown enormously over the past fifty years, without having an impact on income, wealth, and poverty in America. If the basic numbers have not changed over time, including different administrations run by different parties, recessions, wars, and other economic shocks, there are only two conclusions: either the dynamics that control wealth distributions must be independent of the government action taken; or the benefits have been so inefficiently delivered they have had no effect.

To reinforce the point of this chapter only requires a look at the obvious: the income distribution for three widely separated years in American history. (See chart 10) Income for the years 1774, 1860, and 2011 are included. It would be hard to put together three more divergent years than those, so it is hard to argue that the data set is too narrow. The first year, 1774, predated the Declaration of Independence and the Federal government. The second year, 1860, was just prior to the Civil War but the Industrial Revolution was underway. The third year, 2011, reflects contemporary America in the Information Age. Income equality was greater in 1860 than it is now, but 1774 shows the greatest income equality. The related small number of high wage earners and the lack of a mature economy help explain that difference. If income/class ratios remain close to constant over 225 years, then the benefits of welfare state programs are truly invisible.

What do the Charts Mean?

The data in this chapter's charts are puzzling, at least. One would expect that the time and effort Progressives put into mitigating economic inequality would have produced some positive results. Yet we can see there is no discernable impact. This obviously indicates a severe disconnect between the problems and the solutions Progressives put in place to solve them.

Three factors help explain the results: the complexity of the American economy; human behavior; and the dynamics of government service delivery. Any large state economy is exceedingly complex and reacts to the inputs of hundreds of variables. The Federal Reserve and thousands of economists in the private sector spend their careers analyzing the economy's behavior and try to predict what it will do next. The extent of their understanding of the process is more observational than analytical.

Consequently, predictions are little more than guesses. Often economists are way off the mark. For example, they completely missed the beginning of the Great Recession in 2008.

Economies do not follow logic. They do not operate according to the laws of physics, which are measurable and repeatable. Economies receive inputs based on human behavior, which is emotional and unpredictable. Moreover, the inputs are interrelated. When investors sell a stock, its price goes down until buyers appear who want to buy it at the new price. When and why people decide to buy and sell is unpredictable. If the behavior of the economy is too complex to understand, how can anyone predict the benefits that will result from a new government program? Moreover, a dynamic process like the American economy reacts in the same way to inputs that come from new government programs. For example, government-funding effects the federal financial system and job openings affect unemployment. The reaction of the economy to these variables is not known until a program is established.

The second factor is human behavior. Our decision-making places emotion ahead of logic. The results of mass behavior are unpredictable. Here is an example. It is well known that educational attainment correlates very well with income. In other words, people with more education have higher incomes than people who have less education. If the goal of our society is to eliminate wage disparity and provide people with higher incomes, then it would follow that we need to maximize the number or people who graduate from college. However, not everyone goes to college and not everyone who goes to college, graduates. Only 25% of the population has a college degree, currently, so the other 75% do not enjoy the same income opportunities. In a recent survey about attending college, high school students were asked why they chose not to attend college. The reasons given were:

Cannot afford it.

No one in the family has every graduated from college.

Do not know what to major in or what the career should be.

College is too hard.

Do not have time because of work or other responsibilities.

Will not fit in.[27]

Most of those reasons are weak. The first and fourth reasons have validity, the others, less so.

College graduates have higher IQs than the general population so intelligence is certainly a factor (chart provided by the *International Society for Philosophical Enquiry*), but student attitude is another significant variable. Graduation rates at engineering schools are in the range of 50-60%. Since the students accepted to those schools have high intelligence, the ones who leave must do so for reasons other than their capability to do the work. Perhaps they leave because they do not like college or do not have the discipline required to graduate. Perhaps those without those degree-level opportunities include those without the intellectual skill and those without the proper interest level. The notion that the solution to the problem of income level is to send more students to college is specious and does not reflect the realities of post-secondary education.

Another factor regarding college completion and income, is income opportunities in the job market. Of the top fifteen job categories by number of employees for 2015, 61% or twenty-two million jobs require no secondary or post-secondary education. Those include waiters, cashiers, and retail salespeople. If there are fewer jobs that pay a high salary, how can people get jobs in those professions? Politicians are fond of making statements like, "We need more, better paying jobs." Easier said than done. Those better paying jobs come with a college education or a trained technical skill. Lower paying jobs, even if they exist in large numbers, will never provide adequate compensation. Agitation for a higher minimum wage is evidence of that.

The third factor influencing the effectiveness of Progressive efforts toward economic equality is the inefficiency of the government programs themselves. As stated in the prior chapter, bureaucracies, by definition, are inefficient because they comprise groups of individuals executing sets of rules that govern the distribution of money by the government.

If the government sends $ 100 to an individual under a system without rules, that individual receives $ 100. If a bureaucracy is in operation to determine the qualification of individuals before they receive the money, the individual still gets $ 100 but the government pays $ 130 to provide that money, raising the cost of delivering the service. In addition, there is always the problem of fraud. The ability to control fraud depends on the bureaucracies having an eligibility verification system, a recipient verification system, and good enforcement against bad actors. If any one of these three is missing, more lost dollars accumulate along with those lost from bureaucratic inefficiency.

It is clear government needs better ways to deliver services to the public. Traditional programs advocated by the Left do not work; there is ample, unambiguous evidence to verify that. This reality should prompt the Progressives to control their idealistic belief in the academic understanding of the complex problems of society and government's ability to solve them.

CHAPTER FIFTEEN

CONCLUSIONS

Hell is truth seen too late.

Thomas Hobbs

Like all mammals, man had to develop a unique parenting behavior that supported proliferation of his species. Human offspring take a dozen or so years to mature, so parenting skills had to be more complex and provided over a longer time span than other species. The Progressive Gene, with its ultra-caring focus, survived because it offered humans a biological advantage: better parenting skills and increased the odds of offspring survival.

As the morality of man evolved, the strength of a caring gene mattered. It became the centerpiece of the set of moral foundations required to live in the preferred human social group of one hundred individuals. Only a fraction of the population had the Progressive Gene; perhaps 10-15%. The rest of the human population had a weaker version that put them at a disadvantage.

The Progressive Gene has a second moral component, which is also outsized, compared to the general population: drive for fairness. That drive motivates the individual to desire equality, and be intolerant of inequality. Unlike the caring morality, which was useful in parenting, the fairness morality had limited utility in man's primitive social group. Unless you were a male and the tribe leader, your opinions about equality in the group carried no weight.

The Progressive Gene has carried on through human history influencing those who possess it, and pushing them into action. It was unimportant whether it was the advent of agriculture and its impact on the traditional human social group, the emergence of governments with their societal morality, or the changes in government over time as it tried to respond to a changing world, it did not matter. The gene survived through the fall of Rome, the collapse of Europe, the rebirth of monarchies, and the Enlightenment. The gene received its greatest opportunity early in the Industrial Revolution when it was activated by the Enlightenment Project to rail and revolt against the exploitation of human beings working in a mass production society.

The last quarter of the 19th Century and the first third of the 20th Century saw great improvement in the lives of American citizens. It brought expanded voting rights, elimination of political corruption, fair working conditions, and bargaining power against corporations. The welfare state developed to provide services to all citizens in the areas of elder care, retirement benefits, and help for the poor. These activities solidified the playbook for those driven by the Progressive Gene; a playbook that was utilized throughout the Twentieth Century and is still in operation today. The current version centers on the goals of economic and social justice. Achieving these goals is a two-step process; continue to reinterpret the Constitution so it supports government action on behalf of the "exploited", and passing laws that create government programs to provide that support.

The plan is in operation, but is it really working?

The previous chapter presented an array of statistics, which showed that all the programs implemented by the Progressives have done nothing to alleviate critical economic inequality in America. The metrics discussed there are the same ones used by Progressives to rail against capitalism, so they are the ones that matter. However, they have not been able to improve the wealth and income distribution to make it more "fair". They have not made progress in alleviating poverty.

It is not only that their methods have failed. The Progressives are dangerous to the stability of our society because of the harm they cause in seeking their objectives: harm from dividing the nation, distracting us from real problems, and pursuing ideas that are counter to human behavior and desire. How can these criticisms be true when the intentions of the Progressives are so noble? Because their drive to pursue a caring and fairness focused morality makes them blind to reality.

As the model most accurately mirroring what humans want in their government, Democratic Capitalism has emerged from the Darwinian battle of political systems. Theocracies, monarchies, socialist states, and communist states have all failed the test and been discarded.

Fastening a welfare state onto a Capitalist Democracy risks compromising its effectiveness and cripples it for no good reason. Governments operate as systems that mirror the key attributes of human behavior. Those attributes are colored by culture but are the same across all human society: the drive to survive; the will to power; need to control one's life; and the need for respect. A well operating political system must maximize the opportunity for its citizens to achieve these essential goals. An expanding welfare state reduces that opportunity.

Consider what is happening to some of our states today; those teetering on the brink of insolvency. States, as smaller versions of the Federal government, are a good laboratory to show how programs might perform if expanded to the Federal level. If they fail in the states, one would not expect them to succeed in a larger setting. Illinois, a well-publicized example, was unable to balance its budget until recently after a two-year stalemate. The logjam was only broken by passing a $5 billion tax increase. Illinois has unfunded pensions amounting to $120 billion dollars and there is no way to raise taxes enough to cover this deficit. Every time taxes are increased, people leave the state, and they are already leaving at the rate of 100,000 per year. According to a CNBC study (June 2016), there are three states that are worse off than Illinois: Connecticut, Massachusetts, and New Jersey. A GAO estimate, cited in the article, projected those states will have to cut spending or raise taxes by 5% over the next 50 years to remain solvent.

The Victims of Capitalism

Progressives believe that our society is replete with victims of capitalism, so one would expect that dissatisfaction would appear in surveys measuring happiness and satisfaction with life. One of the popular measurement systems for happiness is *The World Happiness Report* (WHR) produced in Canada. The latest results of their research contradict the Progressives' assumption. Apart from the Scandinavian countries and a few others, whose ratings are above seven on a scale of one to ten, the United States earned a score of 6.99 for the year 2016. Our Western European friends are all less happy than we are: Germany, 6.95; the United Kingdom, 6.71; and France, Italy, and Spain, all below Mexico's 6.58. As one might expect, the data correlated well with GDP per capita, social support, life expectancy at birth, and freedom to make life choices, which are fundamental to human life satisfaction. America has all these in abundance.

By and large, Americans are happy with their jobs. Eighty-nine percent say they are satisfied, or very satisfied (Society for Human Resource Management, 2017). Most people learn to accept their career and the income it brings. Some are motivated by job satisfaction, even at lower income levels. Some earn a lot and hate their jobs. Most people do not want money given to them; they prefer a fair chance to earn a living rather than receive government handouts. There is a kind of natural selection that takes place when men and women choose their careers or decide how to make a living. Their choice is driven by aptitude, attitude, and the influence of their family. After high school, most decide to learn a skill or attend college to obtain their professional degree.

Everyone must learn to accept the need to work for a living because a life with safety and security is not possible without income. As the statistics show, people eventually accept the decisions they made. The reality is that higher education is not a universal goal is clear because three-quarters of the individuals facing that choice, go in a different direction.

Who are the Recipients?

Who are the recipients of the Progressive programs for the redistribution of wealth? Do they, in fact, want to participate in this scheme? Most Americans agree that the homeless, hungry, or physically or mentally ill or disabled should receive the benefit of government programs; the widespread, underlying belief is, it is our moral responsibility to help those who can't help themselves. The Progressives go farther. They want to flatten the entire wealth and income distribution: bring up the lower and bring down the higher to achieve economic equality.

How much money would the Progressives transfer to each recipient? A thousand dollars, ten thousand dollars, or a hundred thousand dollars? If they wish to modify the tax system to redistribute wealth, it is important to decide how much to redistribute. What will the recipients of this gift do with the money? Will they use it wisely; perhaps invest it? Will they use the money to raise their standard of living? Will they waste the money on things that don't improve their monetary security? Or will they use their "money gift" in an entirely unique way?

Unearned Government Payments

There is another problem in play and that is the de-motivating effect of getting something for nothing. Human beings have evolved to survive, just like every other species on the planet and because the capabilities of man are widely diverse, the adaptation to survival takes many forms.

Consider the example of dividing the population into those who would survive in the wilderness and those who would not. Those with the drive and motivation put their families and worldly possessions in wagons and set out into an unknown world fraught with danger. Those fearful of that physical challenge, stayed home. The same concept applies to building a business. Starting a business is risky, but may provide a big payoff. Working for someone else would provide stability with fewer benefits. The de-motivating influence of free money is a subversion of the survival mechanism, just like the welfare system of the 1970s, which paid indigent mothers to stay home and have children.

Unearned money is a sensitive issue in America because of our history. America has long been the land of opportunity, of unlimited resources and land that could be worked into something productive. Americans know everyone, except the wealthy, starts in the same place because there is no royalty here. If you work hard and stick to a goal, you'll do ok. It's a choice most, but not all, Americans have.

Arrogant Authority

The arrogance factor plays a part in building the welfare state. What gives the Progressives the right to make decisions for the American people? Are they more qualified than the individual to know what is good for him? This is a common thread throughout the history of the movement. Progressives claim to know better than the rest of us what America needs and they're going to make sure to deliver it. They want to control the environment, control what people eat and drink, control people's weight, control the features on the cars people drive, define the relationships between the sexes, and more.

This is a basic argument about liberty. People on the right have a strong liberty morality, which they use to guard against oppressive authority. The metaphor for this is the Sons of Liberty and the Boston Tea Party. Liberty rejects unwanted authority, which in their view is the concept of a welfare state. In this same context, the Progressives substitute equality for liberty, by opposing institutions (Wall Street) that interfere with equality.

The United States and the World

When the Progressives criticize the American political system, they often state that things are much better in Europe. The say social and economic justice are real, capitalism is reigned in, and people are happier. The impression they want to create is that America is moving backward, or as economist and *New York Times* columnist Paul Krugman put it, "Describing our current era as a new Gilded Age or Belle Époque isn't hyperbole; it's the simple truth." [28]

These kinds of statements misrepresent reality. One look at the GINI coefficient (named for Italian Sociologist Carrado Gini), a commonly accepted measure of economic inequality, reveals the United States is not as equal is its closest friends, but not that different either. In 2014, the United States' GINI score was .394 (zero is perfect equality, 100 is perfect inequality). The Scandinavian countries were in the low .20s and are the historical leaders, France and Germany were near .30, and the UK was at .358. That placed the United States 31% higher than Germany and France. Is this an indicator of a fundamental weakness in our system or a metric that proves nothing when looking at the bigger picture?

In the previous chapter, I described the wealth and income of the top 1% in the United States, with charts clearly showing an increase in inequality since the 1980s. Thomas Piketty, a pioneer in analyzing economic data and its meaning, suggested that phenomenon was due to a retrenchment of professions as the United States moves from a manufacturing and services economy to a high tech economy. The future, built around robots, drones, driverless cars, and the like, will require new skill sets that barely exist today. Piketty's theory is that inequality expands when careers and professions lag behind emerging businesses.

The United States is the world leader in new business creation with a ranking of entrepreneurs that is 15% above the United Kingdom and 22% higher than Germany. Businesses are created faster in the United States than any other country, so career retrenchment and income disruption are also greater. Business creation results in new jobs that reflect the adaptation of American culture to the changes in society; a critical step in keeping pace with other economies of the world.

Are people in Europe happier with their slightly better equality? No. That's because opportunity is more important to people than equality. The United States is an ideal place to build a happy life; still the land of opportunity for all who wish to take advantage of what it offers. America's unique history, geography, and national character call into question comparisons with Europe.

The Republican Image Problem

To create the best government for the American people, it is critical to have two strong political parties operating and working together. In America today, only one party is pushing their narrative every day, the Democrats. The Republicans have control of Congress and have just won the presidency, but they do not exhibit the same vigor. The mainstream media is Left-leaning and more vocal in a polarized climate, because polarization amplifies their message, so the public becomes bombarded with the ideology of the Left. Those on the Right seem content to accept the criticism without a response, but no response validates the accusations as truth. To make matters worse, the Republican Party is also suffering from a broken ideology, unable to unite around a set of principles for governing. It must unite to offer a legitimate alternative to the programs of the Progressives. Our system cannot prosper with an imbalance in political philosophies because governing requires the best ideas from all, not just one side. Furthermore, a philosophical imbalance creates a tyranny of ideas. Americans want a government that can solve problems and that can only happen with consensus.

What is the Future of our Democracy Without a Counterbalance to the Progressives?

Is the American democracy in peril? Like all other political systems, democracies must evolve or they will fail. If American democracy fails, it will not come by revolution, but by the inevitable collapse of economic order caused by insolvency. A decline in the quality of life for all citizens will follow, including those who depend on government programs.

Francis Fukuyama talked about the ways political systems grow or decay in his book *Political Order and Political Decay* (2014). Discussing the welfare state specifically he stated:

> One of the most important challenges facing developed democracies is the unsustainability of their welfare state commitments. The existing social contracts underlying contemporary welfare states were negotiated generations ago when birth rates were higher, people didn't live as long and economic growth was more robust. [Unfortunately], the availability of financing has allowed all modern democracies to push this problem into the future."[29]

Fukuyama added that the resolution of this problem has been hampered by the political polarization that exists in the United States today. The parties compete for campaign funding while their willingness to engage in dialog and negotiation has evaporated. The parties are supposed to use a set of agreed upon rules for negotiation, but they refuse to agree on those rules. When a layer of polarization is on top of our tightly defined system of checks and balances, the county's ability to move forward is blocked.

Our country needs an agreement between the parties that clearly states it is in everyone's best interest to work together. That agreement, however, does not appear to exist. Instead, each party is engaged in a popularity contest to prove its ideology is superior. It will require the American people's anger and desire for change to bring better representation to the federal government.

This book has revealed the story of Progressive thinking: their history; their theory; and their impact on American life. Their position on social justice and equality is morally supportable. All Americans should support equality of opportunity across our land and no American should be denied access to education, job opportunities, or housing in their quest for a comfortable, happy life. Their goal of Economic equality is a different matter. Continued redistribution of wealth with the goal of financing the welfare state will bankrupt the United States, lower the quality of life for Americans, and degrade our political system into a dysfunctional quagmire.

Recent Progressive Adaptation

Over the last couple of decades, there has been a change in the Progressive approach to building the welfare state. New resistance on the part of the federal government to traditional Progressive arguments has dictated this change. In the past, substantive claims were made in support of disadvantaged groups, claiming their inherent rights to support through government action. Over the last two decades, those claims have been rejected by the courts. In response, the Progressives have had to change their arguments and their venues. Their arguments are now based on a utilitarian view of the world: that government needs to enforce laws that guarantee that all receive the same rights. This approach is designed to broaden appeal for the action and increase the odds of success. The venues have changed as Progressives look for better results from state courts.

The Progressives have also come to realize that the past approach has been harmful, because the granting of new group-based rights can interfere with other important rights such as liberty and democracy. This is important deviation from the influence of the Progressive Gene, which tries to keep the focus of interest on caring and fairness. It also shows a crack in the Progressives utopian belief system, because it demonstrates a practical element, which has been missing previously. If the Progressives can better understand the morality of those on the right, American has a better chance to achieve success through a partnership between the Parties and the pursuit of commonly held goals.

Summary

Mankind developed an innate morality over thousands of generations to increase the odds of surviving on earth. That morality continues to be influenced and adapted through childhood development, but retains its basic foundations in adulthood. Its commonly recognized components are distributed unevenly through the population, just like body type and intelligence. For that reason, personal morality is relative and not absolute. Two individuals can have different moralities and be right in their beliefs, based on how they apply those morals in their society.

Man's earliest biological behavior drove him to build a hierarchical social group based on physical strength, but over time that trait was mitigated by the development of weaponry and man's ability to communicate and gain useful information about others. That led to the development of egalitarian tribes who shared common goals. Group members who didn't conform to the rules of the tribe would be killed or ostracized, so they were forced to control their natural urges.

When man developed agriculture, he gained control over his food supply but had to adapt to a new social model that could accommodate large groups living in close proximity. His hierarchical traits returned in the form of social and economic stratification, which led to the formation of governments. This new society possesses its own morality, representing a consensus of its entire people rather than the individual. Those who wanted to become part of society had to accept the rules, laws, and social norms and morality of the group.

Human beings exhibit a spectrum of moral positions that are related to their view of government. At one end of the spectrum sits a group that seeks the status quo and are most comfortable with stability in their lives. At the other end is group seeking change, wanting to improve and advance society to a better place.

Progressives, who desire change, have an outsized proportion of two key moral foundations: caring and fairness. Those foundations drive them to be idealistic about improvements that can be made to society. They see government as the engine necessary to deploy the welfare state, overlooking its inefficiency and ineffectiveness.

The enthusiasm of Progressives must be tempered to move carefully and not cause too much disruption to the greater populace. Otherwise, political instability increases, which impacts the ability of government to operate.

The American society in 2017 is divided on ideological grounds. Political extremism is the norm and that phenomenon, fueled by the twenty-four-hour media, has destroyed compromise, rendering the Federal government impotent. The only way to move the country forward is to return to civil discourse and compromise, because, absent that objective, American society will rot from the inside.

REFERENCES

page 7.   1   *Readers Digest,* May 2013.

page 28.   2   Richard   Wrangham   &   Dale
Peterson, 1996. Houghton-Mifflin, New York, NY.

page 62.   3   T. Jefferson letter to George
Washington, 1793.

page 77.   4   James Madison, May 31st, 1787.
Madison's Notes from the Constitutional Convention,
W.W. Norton, New York, 1966, Page 39.

page 77.   5   James Madison, May 31st, 1787.
Madison's Notes from the Constitutional Convention,
W.W. Norton, New York, 1966, Page 39.

page 79.   6   James Madison, May 31st, 1787.
Madison's Notes from the Constitutional Convention,
W.W. Norton, New York, 1966, Page 39.

page 80.   7   The United States Constitution,
Article 6.

page 81.   8   John Dickinson, April 29, 1788. *Observations on the Constitution as proposed by the Federal Convention*, writing as Fabius VIII. *Philadelphia Mercury* Newspaper, Philadelphia, Pennsylvania.

page 93.   9   Acts of the 5th Congress, 1798.

page 96.   10   James Madison, Federalist number 10, published in The Daily Advertiser November 22, 1787, page 1, and 3.

page 111.   11   Verdict the Margaret Sanger trail (People vs. Byrne, February 3, 1917).

page 117.   12   The Espionage Act, June 15, 1917. 18 U.S.C. chapter. 37 (18 U.S.C. § 792 et seq.).

page 128.   13   Joanne Boydston, 2008. Dewey, *The Early Works*. Southern Illinois University Press.

page 128.   14   John Maynard Keynes, 2016. *The Essential Keynes*. Penguin Classics.

page 137.   15   Lionel Trilling, 1950. Preface: *The Liberal Imagination*, Harcourt, Brace and World.

page 151.   16   Thomas Byrne Edsall, 2004. The Old and New Democratic Parties, a chapter in *Varieties of Progressivism in America,* Edited by Peter Berkowitz, Hoover Institution Press, Stanford University, 2004, Page 32-33.

page 151.   17   Op cit.

page 153.   18   VikingKing, Daily KOS, Blogpost online, February 28th, 2008.

page 157.   19   David Schultz, Twin Cities Daily Planet, Blogpost online, March 24, 2014.

page 161.   20   Frederick Engels, Socialism: Utopian and Scientific, Revue Socialiste, March 1880, Page 6.

page 162.   21   Cassiodorus, On Utopia and Progressive utopian ideals, online, Daily KOS, December 7, 2009.

page 163.   22   Albert Wiggam, 1923. New Decalogue of Science, Indianapolis, Bobbs-Merrill Co.

209

page 163.   23   The New Republic, April 3, 1915.
Page 273.

page 163.   24   John   R.   Commons,   1934.
Institutional Economics: Its place in Political Economy,
Madison, University of Wisconsin Press. Page 874.

page 164.   25   Eugene McCarthy, Time Magazine
February 12, 1979.

page 179.   26   Source   Congressional   Research
Office – US income distribution, December 2016.

page 187.   27   CollegeAtlas.org, *Top six reasons
for   not   attending   college.*
https://www.collegeatlas.org/attending-college.html
February 28, 2017.

page 198.   28   Paul Krugman, Reviewing Capital
in the 21st Century by Thomas Piketty, New York Times
Review of Books, May 8, 2014.

page 200.   29   Fukuyama, Francis. 2011. *Political
Order and Political Decay: From the Industrial
Revolution to the Globalization of Democracy.* New
York: Farrar, Straus, and Giroux, Page 486.

BIBLIOGRAPHY

AZ Quotes. AZQuotes.com. Quotes at the beginning of each chapter.

Barber, Bernard. 1957. *Social Stratification*. New York: Harcourt, Brace & World.

Bell, Daniel. 1973. *The Coming of Post Industrial Society*. New York: Basic Books.

Bellamy, Edward. 1889. *Looking Backward 2000-1887*. Boston: Houghton Mifflin.

Berkowitz, Peter, Ed. 2004. *Varieties of Progressivism in America*. Stanford University: Hoover Institution.

Bohannan, Paul. 1963. *Social Anthropology*. New York: Holt, Rinehart and Winston.

Bowers, Claude G. 1925. *Jefferson and Hamilton: The Struggle for Democracy in America*. Boston and New York: Houghton Mifflin Company.

Cauthen, Kenneth. 1982. *The Passion for Equality*. Totowa, New Jersey: Rowman & Littlefield.

Commager, Henry Steele. 1977. *The Empire of Reason: How Europe Imagined and America Realized the Enlightenment*. Garden City, New York. Anchor/Doubleday.

Conquest, Robert. 2005. *The Dragons of Expectation: Reality and Delusion in the Course of History*. London: W.W. Norton.

Conquest, Robert. 2000. *Reflections of a Ravaged Century.* New York: W.W. Norton.

Croly, Herbert David. 1909. *The Promise of American Life.* New York: The MacMillan Company.

Damasio, Antonio. 2012. *Self Comes to Mind: Constructing the Conscious Brain.* New York: Vintage Books.

Durkheim, Emile. 1984. *The Division of Labor in Society.* New York: The Free Press.

Epstein, Richard. 2006. *How Progressives Re-wrote the Constitution.* Washington D.C: The Cato Institute.

Fukuyama, Francis. 2011. *The Origins of Political Order: From Pre-human Times to the French Revolution.* New York: Farrar, Straus, and Giroux.

Fukuyama, Francis. 2011. *Political Order and Political Decay, from the Industrial Revolution to the Globalization of Democracy.* New York: Farrar, Straus, and Giroux

Gazzaniga, Michael S. 2008. *Human. The Science Behind What Makes Us Unique.* New York: Harper Collins.

Grant, Michael. 1978. *History of Rome.* New York: Charles Scribner's Sons.

Green, Donald, and Shapiro Ira. 1994. *Pathologies of Rational Choice Theory.* New Haven: Yale University Press.

Greene, Thomas. 1974. *Comparative Revolutionary Movements.* New York: Prentice-Hall.

Haidt, Jonathan. 2012. *The Righteous Mind: Why Good People are Divided by Politics and Religion.* New York: Pantheon Books.

Hauser, Marc D. 2006. *Moral minds: How Nature Designed our Universal Sense of Right and Wrong*. New York: Harper Collins.

Hayek, F.A. 2007. *The Road to Serfdom*. London: University of Chicago Press.

Heyrman, Christine Leigh. 1984. *Commerce and Culture: The Maritime Communities of Colonial Massachusetts*. New York: W.W. Norton & Company.

Hughes, John A, Martin, Peter J, and Sharrock, W.W. 1995. *Understanding Classical Sociology*. Thousand Oaks California, Sage.

Johnson, Paul. 1983. *Modern Times: The World from the Twenties to the Eighties*. New York: Harper and Row.

Johnson, Paul. 1977. *Enemies of Society*. London: Weidenfeld & Nicolson.

Kolko, Gabriel. 1962. *Wealth and Power in America: An Analysis of Social Class and Income Distribution*. New York: Frederick A. Praeger.

Kornhauser, William. 1959. *The Politics of Mass Society*. Glencoe, Illinois: The Free Press.

Landtman, Gunnar. 1968. *The Origin of Inequality of the Social Classes*. New York: Greenwood Press.

Libertyinsight.com (2013 https://libertyinsight.com/2013/02/28/chart-of-the-week-federal-spending-and-the-sequester/

Link, Arthur S. 1967. *American Epoch: A History of the United States Since the 1890s*. New York: Alfred A. Knopf.

Lipset, Seymour Martin. 1963. *The First New Nation: The United States in Historical and Comparative Perspective.* London: Heinemann.

Locke, John. 1790. *The Second Treatise of Government.* Free of Copyright.

Madison, James. 1966. *Notes on the Debates in the Federal Convention of 1787.* New York. W.W. Norton.

Mann, Arthur, Ed. 1975. *The Progressive Era: Major Issues of Interpretation.* Hinsdale, Illinois: Dryden Press.

Mann, Arthur, Ed. 1963. *The Progressive Era: Liberal Renaissance or Liberal Failure.* New York: Holt, Rinehart and Winston.

Marx, Karl. 2012. *Das Kapital.* Chicago: Dragan Nicolic, Aristeus Books.

McDonald, Forrest. 1985. *Novus Ordo Seclorum: The Intellectual Origins of the Constitution.* Lawrence, Kansas. University of Kansas Press.

Mignet, F.A.M. 1912. *History of the French Revolution 1789-1814.* London: G. Bell.

Nettels, Curtis P. 1963. *The Roots of American Civilization: A History of American Colonial Life.* New York: Appleton-Century-Crofts.

Olson, Mancur. 1982. *The Rise and Decline of Nations: Economic Growth, Stagflation, and Social Rigidities.* New Haven: Yale University Press.

Phillips, Kevin. 2002. *Wealth and Democracy.* New York: Broadway Books.

Pinker, Steven. 2002. *The Blank Slate: The Modern Denial of Human Nature.* New York: Penguin Putnam.

Pipes, Richard. 1999. *Property and Freedom.* New York: Alfred A. Knopf.

Piketty, Thomas, EHESS, and CPREMAP Paris, Emmanuel Saez, Harvard University, and NBER. Income Inequality in the United States. July 2001.

Samuels, Andrew. 1993. *The Political Psyche.* London: Routledge Press.

Saez, Emmanuel. 2016. *Striking it Richer: The Evolution of Top Incomes in the United States.* Berkeley: UC Berkeley.

Sandel, Michael J. 2009. *Justice: What's the Right Thing to Do?* New York: Farrar, Straus, and Giroux.

Schoen, John W. *Three states are a bigger fiscal mess than Illinois.* CNBC, June 1, 2016.

Scullard, H.H. 2000. *A History of the Roman World 753 to 146 BC.* London: Routledge Press.

Scullard, H.H. 2007. *A History of Rome from the Gracchi to Nero.* London: Routledge Press.

Sen, Amartya. 1999. *Development as Freedom.* New York: Anchor Books.

Service, Elman R. 1962. *Primitive Social Organization. An Evolutionary Perspective.* New York: Random House.

Service, Elman R. 1975. *The Origins of the State and Civilization. The Process of Cultural Evolution.* New York: W.W. Norton.

Shapiro, Ian. 2003. *The Moral Foundations of Politics.* New Haven: Yale University Press.

Skowronek, Stephen. 1993. *The Politics Presidents Make: Leadership from John Adams to Bill Clinton.* Cambridge: Belknap Press.

Starr, Chester G. 1991. *History of the Ancient World.* Oxford: Oxford University Press.

Starr, Chester G. 1961. *Origins of the Greek Civilization.* New York: Alfred A. Knopf.

Stiglitz, Joseph, E. 2013. *The Price of Inequality. How Today's Divided Society Endangers Our Future.* New York: W.W. Norton.

Shweder, Richard, Minow, Martha, and Markus, Hazel Rose, Eds. 2002. *Engaging Cultural Differences. The Multicultural Challenge in Liberal Democracies.* New York: The Russell Sage Foundation.

Tindall, George Brown. 1988. *America: A Narrative History* Volume 1. New York: W.W. Norton.

Tocqueville De, Alexis. 2004. *Democracy in America.* New York: Library Classics.

Turiel, Elliot. 2002. *The Culture of Morality.* Cambridge: Cambridge University Press.

US Bureau of Labor Statistics (2012) data. http://www.truthfulpolitics.com/http:/truthfulpolitics.com/comments/u-s-federal-government-employment-president-political-party/?utm_source=twitter&utm_medium=friendly%2Blinks&utm_campaign=twitter%2Bfl%2Bplugin

US Census Bureau (2015), Current Population Survey, https://www.census.gov/data/tables/time-series/demo/income-poverty/historical-poverty-people.html.

US GovernmentSpending.com
http://www.gao.gov/financial_pdfs/fy2007/guide.pdf

Wrangham, Richard W. & Peterson, Dale. (1996). *Apes and the Origin of Human Violence.* New York, Houghton-Mifflin.

World Economic Forum (WEF), *US Social Mobility may be Even Worse Than You Thought.* 10 October 2016. https://www.weforum.org/agenda/2016/10/us-social-mobility-might-be-even-worse-than-you-thought

82832396R00130

Made in the USA
Columbia, SC
06 December 2017